T0272726

*un*CONSTRAINED

loving God with abandon

Kyle McNutt

Carpenter's Son Publishing

Unconstrained: Loving God with Abandon

©2018 by Kyle McNutt

Published by Carpenter's Son Publishing, Franklin, Tennessee

Published in association with Larry Carpenter of Christian Book Services, LLC
www.christianbookservices.com

Edited by Robert Irvin

Cover and Interior Design by Suzanne Lawing

Printed in the United States of America

978-1-946889-59-1

Contents

Acknowledgments

As you might imagine with a book that has taken nearly a decade to complete, there are a significant number of people who have either directly participated in its creation or inspired me along the way. There are some who have done both. And then there are all of those who have made a lasting impact on my heart over my forty-year journey of life—people whose influence undoubtedly surfaces throughout this book. Obviously, I cannot include everyone whose friendship I deeply cherish here, which causes some hesitancy in wanting to include acknowledgments of any kind. That said, there are certain folks I would be remiss not to mention by name, so please allow me to express my thanks to a few . . .

Words cannot begin to express the gratitude that wells up in my heart when I consider the blessing God has bestowed in placing me in the family He so lovingly chose. Carey, you are my perfect partner in this life, the one through whom the Holy Spirit reveals so much of the depth of passion in the Father's heart, both for me and for others. You so beautifully embody the servant's heart of Jesus, and I am still a little perplexed as to why you said yes to a knucklehead like me. But I'm glad you did! Brooklyn and Ashtyn: oh, how I love getting to be your daddy! Your joy keeps me young, your curiosity keeps me learning, and your love keeps me wanting to be a better man. Keep your eyes on Jesus, sweet girls. He is the only one who will never let you down. To the rest of the family, McNutts, Taylors, McCulloughs, and Richardsons: thank you for believing in me and investing your love, prayers, time, energy, money, and God-only-knows-what-else into my life. Each of you have impacted me greatly, and I am truly blessed to call you all family.

Mike Bickle, Allen Hood, Misty Edwards, and the rest of the crew at the International House of Prayer in Kansas City: the example you set and the truths you have shared over the last fourteen years have completely revolutionized the way I view and relate to Jesus. Thank you for your faithfulness, even in the dry and difficult times. And thank you for challenging a twentysomething-year-old youth pastor more than a decade ago to abandon complacent, "bare minimum" Christianity in order to pursue Jesus with extravagance and abandon. I still have miles to go, but knowing that He loves me, even in my weakness, propels me ever onward. Thank you for sharing that life-altering truth!

Penny Simmons, Doug Stone, Linda Motlong, Michel Castro, Richard King, and the rest of our Lubbock International House of Prayer family: thank you for stretching and encouraging Carey and I as we first began learning what it looked like to embrace a lifestyle of prayer, fasting, the prophetic, and a million other things that were brand new to us. The LIHOP community is so precious to us, and it was such an integral part in God's plan for growing and maturing us. What great friends and memories!

Pastors Todd and Trish Turnbow: thank you for being a steady voice of encouragement in my life. So many times you have spoken a word from the Lord to me that came at exactly the right time, communicating with such love and grace that my heart was able to receive the truth and allow it to change me. No matter where life leads us, Carey and I will always consider you guys to be our pastors. More importantly, I am thankful I get to call you friends.

Ben Donley, you were the first one with whom I shared a portion of my manuscript for this book, and your feedback and encouragement to "just keep writing" is one of the primary reasons you are holding this book today. I miss our hangout times and our boneheaded, late-night conversations over a game of QB1. Pass back right, and down with the Yankees!

I am blessed to have had the opportunity to sit under the teaching and leadership of a number of great pastors and mentors over the past couple of decades, some who have influenced me from afar, and many who have become close, personal friends. In chronological order of when our paths crossed (to the best of my recollection): Pastor Doug Halcomb, Pastor Pat Brown, Will and Anne Baker, Pastor Mickey and Bonnie Eckles, Pastor Mike and Kim Cox, Pastor Ray and Nanette Hill, Pastor Randal and Andrea Ross, Pastor J.J. and Brandi Hefley, Pastor Chuck and Ann Williams, Merryl Carson, Pastor Steve and Marci Fish, and Pastor Robert and Debbie Morris: my life and my eternity are forever changed as a result of your faithfulness. Thank you doesn't really suffice, but it's the best I can do here!

So many friends, many who have become like family, have been a huge part of our lives and ministry over the past decade or more. And then there are more recent friends who have either assisted directly with this book or offered significant encouragement along the way. It is impossible for me to feel good about a list of acknowledgments that doesn't include the following names: Justin and Marla Barnard, Ellis and Cindy Dean, Maci Dean, Amie Dean, David and Toni Ridley, Justin and Mindy Lentz, Lance and Lori Matthews, Kelsi Davis, Autumn Matthews, Reagan Matthews, Rick and Holly Betenbough, Ron and Connie Betenbough, Jonathan and Hannah Taussig, Don and Judy Cooper, Ben and Stephanie Donley, Dale and Johanna Waterhouse, Shane and Dijon Russell, Greg and Angie Storm, Ashley Bird, Ben Waters, Todd Knowlton, Brad and Amy Stroup, Brian and Jenny Findley, Brian Maines, Corey and Tara Harmon, Bruce and Ruth

Menefee, Bryan Peterson, Chris and Amber White, Shawn and Tiffany Hall, Shane and Beth Barnard, Doug Garrett, Steve and Lisa Dirks, Jessika Tate, Jill Hurley, Jennifer Beamer, Dr. Frank and Janet Babb, Joel and Heather Bryant, Tim and Rory Aughinbaugh, Julie Dagle, Aaron and Kelli Mills, Ben and Liz Fritz, Heath and Tara Klein, and Melinda Etheridge. Some of you offered direct encouragement and assistance with this project, and some have inspired me indirectly through your service, creativity or ministry, but all of you have encouraged me with your love and friendship!

Thank you to Larry Carpenter, Suzanne Lawing, Bob Irvin, and the rest of the team at Carpenter's Son Publishing for helping me take this project from a completed manuscript to an actual book! At the exact time that I began to wonder if this project would ever become a reality, God saw to it to make sure our paths crossed. Your expertise has been invaluable, and I sincerely hope I get the opportunity to work with you on future projects.

There is a 100 percent chance I have left someone off this list who is going to become an obvious omission to me as soon as the book goes to print. Please accept my sincerest apologies in advance! Without a doubt, this section has been the most difficult one in the book to write.

Let me close by saying, to all who have stuck by me through the years, despite my many phases, inconsistencies, and lapses of self-control, I have given you every excuse under the sun to walk away and find better company. Thank you for sticking around. I'm certain I will provide you with plenty more opportunities to change your mind, but I hope you will continue to display the same patience and longsuffering that you have thus far.

Grace and peace to you all . . .

Kyle McNutt

Foreword

When I was five years old, I experienced a single, life-altering event that would affect every decision I would make for the next thirty-six years.

As a young child, I lived with my mother and little sister in Midland, Texas. My father was a heroin addict and convicted criminal who abandoned our family when I was about eighteen months old. My mom met another man, and when I was five, she relocated our little family to the small West Texas town so she could be with him.

One sunny Saturday afternoon, I decided to do what any little five-year-old girl in a new location would—I set out to explore and enjoy the country lifestyle to which we now belonged. My mom's new boyfriend lived in a travel trailer on his parents' property on the outskirts of town, and on that property they had a number of chickens. Being a curious child, I just couldn't resist grabbing and inspecting the eggs that were so readily available, and as you might expect, this led to a cacophony of loud squawking from the mother hens. It also led to severe disciplinary action from the new man in our lives. I can still remember it like it was yesterday—dangling from his firm grip by one arm, screaming at the top of my lungs while he smacked and berated me. It was bad, but the worst was yet to come.

After the dramatic events of the afternoon, I lie awake in the darkness of the travel trailer, listening as my mother and her new man argued about the discipline he had meted out. I could hear the frustration in his voice begin to escalate, not realizing that the next couple of minutes would become a defining moment in my young soul. "You have to pick," he said. "It's either her or me. You have to choose." I laid there trying to pretend I was asleep, but complete terror came over my five-year-old heart as I waited to hear how my mother would answer. *Surely, she'll choose me,* I thought. *Won't she?* My heart pounded in my chest and my mouth went dry as I laid beside my little sister, striving with all my might to lay motionless and not stir up any additional conflict. Suddenly, the response came. "Can't you just tolerate her?!"

In a split-second, a lie was birthed, and an innocent child would believe for the next thirty-six years that she was unloved, unwanted, and only intended to be *tolerated.* This single event set me on a journey of searching for, accepting, and offering a perverted version of "love" to every male counterpart that would give me the attention I so desperately desired. Each decision I would make from that moment on was rooted in a desire to be seen as beautiful, desirable, and worthy of someone's love, even if it was only a false and twisted version of the real thing. In my eyes, my value had been reduced to nothing, so I began self-medicating with premarital sex and alcohol, all while begging others to take notice of and ascribe worth to my broken heart.

When I eventually became willing to honestly evaluate the root cause of the unhealed pain inside my soul, I asked the Lord to take me back to the exact moment that I had embraced the lie that I was unlovable. I knew that in order to finally move beyond its disastrous effects, I would be forced to confront my entire belief system head on, combating the lie I had accepted with the truth of God's love. I knew that I was in for a great deal of searching, surrendering, and believing if a breakthrough was going to come, and that proved to be 100 percent true. But when I encountered the reality of the Bridegroom God, my life was forever changed! Not only am I loved, I am *extravagantly* loved, and I am now able to receive that love without suspicion. Words cannot describe the freedom I continue to experience as I am learning to give and receive love according to God's definition and plan!

In *Unconstrained: Loving God with Abandon,* Kyle McNutt blows the lid off the enemy's lie that we must perform, strive for, and earn God's unconditional love. His words provoke the reader's heart to ask: "What if I actually am loved perfectly, even though I have done nothing to deserve it? And what if, in accepting that love, I can finally be free to give love in return, fully and with total abandon?"

Kyle teaches us with such humility, but with certain resolve, that we are all capable of experiencing intimacy with Jesus that can only be likened to the surrender, vulnerability, and expectancy of a brand-new bride awaiting the sacred union of covenant with her bridegroom. In fact, we are not only all capable of experiencing this depth of relationship with God, we are *intended* to experience it!

When I think of the bondage in my own life that ensued from childhood, I wish a million times over that someone would have shared with me what Kyle is shouting from the rooftops in this revelatory book. The Father desires to move us from an enslavement mindset to a position of sonship. Jesus longs to shatter our prostitution paradigm of "love" as we enter into a fully devoted bridal partnership with His heart. We have an enemy who is obsessed with keeping us from walking in either of these two great realities, and in this book, Kyle walks us through every lie and trap that Satan has laid for us and smashes them with truth that will forever change the way we receive and give love—unconstrained and completely abandoned.

Pastor Trish Turnbow
Lead Pastor and Founder of 414 Missions
The Worship Center, Lubbock, Texas

Introduction

RETURNING TO OUR FIRST LOVE

Hello, my name is Kyle, and I am a recovering church basher. I feel I need to begin a book like this with that simple confession. After all, the book you are holding is all about growing in love, and while the primary focus is on loving God, we cannot possibly get away from the reality of God's incredible love for His church. Therefore, I am not proud of the confession I am making, as I know my less-than-constructive criticisms of the church have broken my Lord's heart on numerous occasions. While I truly believe that the roots of my angst can be found in an at least somewhat holy discontentment resulting from the way we, as followers of Jesus, have settled for less than the "life more abundantly" that He promised us, I still cannot help but feel remorse for throwing mud on the bride that Jesus loves so passionately.

The reason I feel the need to tell you this before diving in is twofold. First, if you are a church basher like I have been, I want to gently encourage you to *stop it right now!* Repent and ask the Lord to allow you to see the church the way He does.

While we are far from perfect, the Lord is able to see what it is we are guaranteed to become as a result of the finished work of Christ. Actually, He sees what it is that He has already made us to be. Our hearts, minds, and lifestyles simply have some catching up to do!

Second, if you have never found yourself with even an inkling of the "holy discontentment" of which I speak, I encourage you to take some time to look around and make some difficult evaluations. While we must be careful of the comments we make regarding the church (the church is the people, remember?), the institution that we have come to accept as "church" is not only imperfect, but it is also not justified, sanctified, or redeemed. It not only deserves, but also requires, our strictest evaluation. Somehow, in the two thousand years of church history, we have often come to accept buildings, programs, services, service projects, cookouts, concerts, and the like as "church." While there is nothing inherently wrong with any of these things, I fear that we have been somewhat blinded to the reality of what should set a community of Christ followers apart from the rest of the world. While Jesus has called us out of the world to be countercultural, we have instead settled for notching out our own "Christian" subculture that can exist easily in the context of mainstream, secular society.

THERE IS ONE THING, AND ONE THING ALONE, WHICH SEPARATES US FROM THE WORLD AROUND US, AND THAT IS THE INDWELLING PRESENCE OF THE HOLY SPIRIT— GOD DWELLING IN AND AMONG US.

There is one thing, and one thing alone, which separates us from the world around us, and that is the indwelling presence of the Holy Spirit—God dwelling in and among us. Shouldn't that be enough to capture our attention and command our energies? Do we really need the bright lights and smoke machines (although there is nothing inherently wrong with either)? Shouldn't our fellowship times include more than grilling hot dogs and tossing horseshoes? Don't we have more to offer the world than just our vain attempts to be "cutting edge" and "culturally relevant?" More importantly, don't we owe it to the One who created us and loves us completely for it to be "all about Him" in reality, and not just in a cute mantra we recite in our prayers and worship choruses?

Is it possible that, like the church in Ephesus, we have lost our first love in our pursuit of good deeds, hard work, and excellence in ministry? To the degree that we have, we are in severe danger. It is critical that we make an honest, prayerful evaluation of our lives, both personally and corporately, and then make the necessary adjustments, lest Jesus come to us quickly and remove our lampstand from its place (Revelation 2:4-5).

The primary purpose of this book is to call all of us who desire to be disciples of Jesus to recapture our first love and embrace the simple yet difficult commands He makes: "'And you shall love the Lord your God with all your heart, with all your soul, with all your mind, and with all your strength. . . . You shall love your neighbor as yourself'" (Mark 12:30-31). I believe wholeheartedly that God is restoring these great commandments to first place in the life of His church. He will have it no other way! In fact, I believe that Jesus was speaking prophetically about His church at the end of the age when He shared these commandments with His listeners. When He says, "You shall," He is not only saying, "This is something that you should do," but He is also saying, "This is going to happen. You *shall*, in due time. I guarantee it!" What an incredible reality—the One who gives the commandments is the same One who gives the grace and ability to fulfill them!

Many of us have allowed ourselves to be distracted and lulled to sleep, and the only thing that will awaken the sleeping giant is a recapturing of the knowledge of the One who has called us out of darkness and into the light. We are so tempted to give our attention to lesser things, and when we do, the result is a church devoid of power and passion. Moreover, those of us who have worn ourselves out by trying to break free from our slumbering states have most often focused on treating symptoms rather than curing the deeper cause of our illnesses. In his book *The Knowledge of the Holy*, A.W. Tozer states:

> The Church has surrendered her once lofty concept of God and has substituted for it one so low, so ignoble, as to be utterly unworthy of thinking, worshiping men. This she has done not deliberately, but little by little and without her knowledge; and her very unawareness only makes her situation all the more tragic. The low view of God entertained almost universally among Christians is the cause of a hundred lesser evils everywhere among us.[1]

Striving to be free of sin is noble, but it will never provide us with the strength we need to endure. Serving the poor in our communities is admirable and necessary, but without the knowledge and power of God at work within us, we can do little more than simply give handouts. Working harder and ministering more effectively is not (and never will be) the answer. The cure to all that ails us is found only in knowing and loving God. That is why the Apostle Paul prayed that the church in Ephesus would experience "the Spirit of wisdom and revelation, so that [they] may know Him better" (Ephesians 1:17). As a church that has lost its first love, we

---

[1] A.W. Tozer, *The Knowledge of the Holy* (New York: HarperOne, 1961), vii.

too must have an encounter with His Spirit so that our hearts may be brought to life and we may be "strengthened with might through his Spirit in the inner man" (Ephesians 3:16).

In short, our reason for existing, and the only way we will ever have an eternal impact on the world around us, is found in allowing the Holy Spirit to work in our hearts to produce love for Jesus. Out of the overflow that comes from experiencing this place of intimacy, we will be empowered to truly love and serve those around us. However, before we can really offer the fullness of our love to God, it is essential that we grasp, at least at some level, the reality of His incredible love for us. After all, John, Jesus' beloved disciple, tells us, "We love Him because He first loved us" (1 John 4:19). We are empowered to love God and to love others only by first understanding and walking in the love God has for us. So it seems to me that this is the best place to begin. I invite you to take the journey with me—that is, if you don't mind associating with an imperfect, recovering church basher.

May the grace and peace of the Father be yours as you grow in your knowledge of and love for Jesus.

Chapter One

THE RAVISHED HEART OF GOD

"[I]n its deepest mystery, all of salvation history is in fact
a divine love story between Creator and creature, between
God and Israel, a story that comes to its climax on the
bloody wood of a Roman cross."

–Brant Pitre, Jesus the Bridegroom:
The Greatest Love Story Ever Told[2]

When you think about God, what is the primary image that
comes to mind? Don't think about it too long or too hard, lest
you ruin the experiment. I am not asking you to refer to the
volumes of material you have stored away from sermons you
have heard or classes you have attended. In fact, please don't
attempt to do this. I simply want to know what immediately
comes to mind when someone mentions God to you. More

---

[2] Brant Pitre, *Jesus the Bridegroom: The Greatest Love Story Ever Told* (New
York: Image, 2014), 3.

importantly, I want *you* to know what immediately comes to your mind. For some of us, this exercise is more difficult than for others, as most of us probably have not spent much time thinking about God at all. As tragic as this is, it is the subject of another book. For now, even if it takes a moment, honestly evaluate your thoughts regarding the Lord.

Obviously, your picture of God is going to be heavily determined by your life experiences, including both your firsthand experience and what you have heard from others. Maybe you approach God primarily as a king. Whether this is a positive or negative image in your mind, you have come to identify God primarily by His bigness and sovereignty. This is a valid and true (although partial) representation of the Lord that is clearly spelled out in the Scriptures. In 1 Timothy 1:17, Paul writes, "Now to the King eternal, immortal, invisible, to God who alone is wise, be honor and glory for ever and ever. Amen." He is the King, and He is seated on His throne. If this is your primary identification of God, then rest assured that you are on to something!

Another popular (albeit significantly less Scriptural) image of God is that of a loving grandfather—someone who is there to pat our heads, tell us how great we are, and make sure we have everything we need (or want). While there is no doubt that God is loving, His love does not always take the warm and fuzzy form that this image conjures up. God is our number one encourager, but He will not lie to us and tell us how great we are. In fact, to the contrary, His Word makes it clear how far from "great" we are apart from Jesus' completed work on the cross. God has also promised to take care of our needs; however, what we *think* we need and what we *actually* need are often far removed from one another. In addition, I have learned over the years that God has very little concern for our comfort. Although I am a huge fan of Charles Wesley's hymn, "Gentle Jesus, Meek and Mild," He often looks a lot more like "harsh Jesus, mean and wild!" He calls us to "take up our cross and follow Him" (Mark 8:34), knowing this will cost us everything, perhaps including our safety, or even our lives. So although God is our Father, maybe we need to rethink this "heavenly grandfather" image.

My experience has been that many people view God primarily as a judge. This can be a very accurate, scriptural view of God, depending upon what connotations this identification carries with it. Most of us, if we are honest, would probably admit that when we think of God as being a judge, we view Him as someone who is waiting for us to screw things up so He can take us out. We associate Him with the moody, crotchety "Judge Judy" image, which could not possibly be further from the truth! God is a righteous judge who is committed to revealing and judging sin in the lives of both believers and nonbelievers. He desires to remove everything that hinders love, and He is passionate about doing so.

> MOST OF US, IF WE ARE HONEST, WOULD PROBABLY ADMIT THAT WHEN WE THINK OF GOD AS BEING A JUDGE, WE VIEW HIM AS SOMEONE WHO IS WAITING FOR US TO SCREW THINGS UP SO HE CAN TAKE US OUT.

Make no mistake; there is an element of fear involved here. In Luke 12:4-5, Jesus tells us, "'And I say to you, My friends, do not be afraid of those who kill the body, and after that have no more that they can do. But I will show you whom you should fear: Fear Him who, after He has killed, has power to cast into hell; yes, I say to you, fear Him!'" However, our fear of the Lord must be tempered with an understanding of His great love for us. Romans 2:4 tells us that it is the kindness of God that leads us to repentance. Although He is a judge, He is a kind judge who desires each of us to agree with Him and come to a place of repentance and knowledge of the truth (1 Timothy 2:4). Yes, it is true that God will allow those who choose to ignore His voice and reject the sacrifice of Jesus to spend eternity in Hell, but I believe that He is heartbroken over each one who makes that choice. He is the Judge who desires to show mercy, and He takes every opportunity to lavish that mercy upon us.

Whatever your primary image of God might be, you can bet that, at least to some degree, that identification has been shaped by your interactions with others who may fit that description. For example, if you view God primarily as Father, and you have a good relationship with your earthly father, then you likely have a fairly positive image of God. However, if your earthly father is (or was) abusive, or even simply absent from your life, then the emotions created by your situation will also carry over into your relationship with God. The point I am trying to make is that due to our different life experiences and encounters with God, if you were to ask a room full of one hundred people to explain their views of who God is, then you would likely get a hundred different answers. This is extremely interesting when you consider that our view of God is a primary determinant of how we experience Him in our daily lives!

The Bridal Paradigm

In this chapter, I would like to introduce you to a paradigm, or a view of God, that you might not be familiar with, or at least that you may not have considered at length—the reality of Jesus as a bridegroom who is passionately in love with His bride, the church. This is a view of God which is established throughout the Scriptures, both in the Old and New Testaments. It is nothing new, but it is a truth about God that I believe He is emphasizing at this particular time in history.

I realize that when you start talking about brides, grooms,

and weddings that there is a tendency for many ladies to get excited and for most men to quickly shut down and tune out. With that said, I invite you to stay with me for a few minutes regardless of your gender, because the subject of the bridegroom is for both men and women. In fact, it actually has nothing to do with gender. So, men, you can breathe a sigh of relief: you will not be required to put on a wedding dress, buy flowers, or cry.

When the Bible refers to Christ followers as the "bride of Christ," it is speaking of a position of intimacy that no other created being can experience with the bridegroom. There are times when the Bible refers to both men and women as "sons of God," which simply refers to a position of authority and the believer's standing as an heir of God. In the same way, when the Bible refers to believers as the "bride of Christ," it speaks of a position of intimacy with God that goes beyond simple friendship.

Before we continue, it is important to point out that when we discuss the topic of intimacy with God, we must remove any connotations of physical intimacy or the skewed view of intimacy that the world accepts as reality. The intimacy that I am speaking of here goes much deeper and exists on a spiritual level that cannot be experienced in human relationships. It is an active intimacy with the heart of God in which we are motivated by the movements of His heart, and He responds to the movements of ours. It is a beautiful reality that is available to all who would say yes to Jesus!

The essence of the bridal paradigm is summed up beautifully by the Apostle Paul in 1 Corinthians 2:9-12:

That is what the Scriptures mean when they say, "No eye has seen, no ear has heard, and no mind has imagined what God has prepared for those who love him." But it was to us that God revealed these things by his

Spirit. For his Spirit searches out everything and shows us God's deep secrets. No one can know a person's thoughts except that person's own spirit, and no one can know God's thoughts except God's own Spirit. And we have received God's Spirit (not the world's spirit), so we can know the wonderful things God has freely given us (NLT).

God has prepared things for those of us who say yes to Him that are so incredible we cannot even begin to imagine them in our wildest dreams! Paul tells us that *no* eye, *no* ear, and *no* mind can comprehend the fullness of what God wants to share with His bride. I can dream up some pretty mind-blowing scenarios related to who God is, what He wants to accomplish, and what Heaven on earth looks like, but my thoughts pale in comparison to the reality that exists in the heart and mind of the Father.

Once he has made it abundantly clear that we cannot possibly conjure up even an inkling of the magnificence and beauty of God's heart, Paul shares with us that the Holy Spirit takes God's secrets and desires to make them known to those who would search them out. It is interesting to think about the fact that God has emotions, feelings, and secrets, but it absolutely renders me speechless to think that He wants to make them known to me! God actually desires for us to know Him intimately, to know the deepest realities of His heart that are most important to Him. He is very careful with these thoughts and feelings, and He does not make them known to everyone. He reveals the fullness of His heart only to those who have His Spirit living inside them. While this type of relationship is available to everyone, only those who have made Jesus their forgiver and leader will ever experience this encounter with the Spirit of wisdom and revelation that empowers us to know and love God more fully (Ephesians 1:17).

One of the deepest secrets of God's heart that the Holy

Spirit longs to emphasize to the church is that He is *ravished* with burning desire for those who would give their lives in devotion to Him! The prophet Isaiah spoke to the nation of Israel, as recorded in Isaiah 62:1-5:

> For Zion's sake I will not keep silent, for Jerusalem's sake I will not remain quiet, till her [righteousness] shines out like the dawn, her salvation like a blazing torch. The nations will see your [righteousness], and all kings your glory; you will be called by a new name that the mouth of the Lord will bestow. You will be a crown of splendor in the Lord's hand, a royal diadem in the hand of your God. No longer will they call you Deserted, or name your land Desolate. But you will be called Hephzibah, and your land Beulah; for the Lord will take delight in you, and your land will be married. As a young man marries a young woman, so will your Builder marry you; as a bridegroom rejoices over his bride, so will your God rejoice over you (NIV).

ONE OF THE DEEPEST SECRETS OF GOD'S HEART THAT THE HOLY SPIRIT LONGS TO EMPHASIZE TO THE CHURCH IS THAT HE IS *RAVISHED* WITH BURNING DESIRE FOR THOSE WHO WOULD GIVE THEIR LIVES IN DEVOTION TO HIM!

Keep in mind that in this passage God is speaking a prophecy to the nation of Israel, His chosen people. While I believe wholeheartedly that many of the prophetic promises of the Old Testament were intended for—and are only completely fulfilled in and through—the nation of Israel, this passage reveals the heart of the Father for all who have been "grafted in" (Romans 11:17). The truth revealed in this passage is firmly established throughout the Scriptures, including

Paul's letters addressed specifically to Gentile believers.

That said, if you are at all like me, your response after reading that passage for the first time is probably "Huh? What in the world is Hephzibah? Should I consider it a compliment to be called that?" Well, it might help to read verse 4 again, this time from a translation that actually translates the words: "Never again will you be called the Godforsaken City or the Desolate Land. Your new name will be the City of God's Delight and the Bride of God, for the Lord delights in you and will claim you as His own" (NLT). We can see from this translation that when God refers to His people as Hephzibah or Beulah, He is actually calling us "the city of God's delight" or "the Bride of God." He sees us as His bride!

Relentless Pursuit

In my opinion, there is no single place in Scripture where God's ravished heart for His bride is more clearly revealed than in the book of Hosea. While I will provide a very short summary of the first few chapters of Hosea, I would strongly encourage you to read the original text and allow the Holy Spirit to speak directly to your heart regarding the depths of God's love for His church.

In chapter 1, the prophet Hosea tells us that the Lord speaks to him and instructs him to go down to what we might call the "red light district" of Israel. Once he arrives, he is to find and marry a prostitute. Not only is he to marry this lady of the evening, he is to love her—to take her into his home and heart. And to make things worse, as if that were possible, her name is Gomer! If I am Hosea, I am sad to admit that the story likely falls apart at this point, and I can only imagine that a good Jewish man like Hosea might have struggled, at least a bit, with what he heard from the Lord. All that we are told in the text is that Hosea obeyed the word of the Lord, but

I have to assume that this was a "You want me to do *what?!?!*" moment for Hosea, if not aloud, then at least in his heart and mind. But as is often the case, God had more in mind here than just the comfort and religious tradition of the one whom He called.

God's command to Hosea was to serve as an example of how God had loved His people, even though they had made whores of themselves, committing adultery against Him by worshiping other gods. Hosea seeks out and marries this prostitute named Gomer, and she is apparently very good at her occupation. The Scriptures tell us that during Hosea's marriage to Gomer she bears some children, and Hosea was not involved in the process! She continues to prostitute herself even while they are married.

At this point in the story, we can only assume that Hosea's ministry did not begin quite as he had expected or desired. However, he is partnering with God to deliver a critical message to the people of Israel. Through Hosea, God makes it clear that His people have cut themselves off from Him, but that He will continue to pursue them with the hope that they will wholeheartedly return to Him. Listen to the heart of the bridegroom, as revealed in Hosea 2:6-8:

> "For this reason I will fence her in with thornbushes. I will block her path with a wall to make her lose her way. When she runs after her lovers, she won't be able to catch them. She will search for them but not find them. Then she will think, 'I might as well return to my husband because I was better off with him than I am now.' She doesn't realize it was I who gave her everything she has—the grain, the new wine, the olive oil; I even gave her silver and gold. But she gave all my gifts to Baal" (NLT).

Can you sense the broken heart of the Lover of our souls as

He reveals His plans for pursuit? Reading this passage, I can't help but attempt to imagine how I might feel if I were in God's place. Let's say that I was to give my wife a beautiful gold bracelet, only to find out later that she had traded it in for a new gold watch that she gave to another man. Although I am convinced this would never happen, I know that if it did I would be devastated! It would not be because she did not care enough about the bracelet to keep it, but because she had given her heart to another when, as a result of our marriage covenant, I was the only one deserving of her affections. Given that God's capacity to love is infinitely larger than ours, how much His heart must hurt when we not only give our worship to another, but we use the very gifts He has given us in order to do so!

GIVEN THAT GOD'S CAPACITY TO LOVE IS INFINITELY LARGER THAN OURS, HOW MUCH HIS HEART MUST HURT WHEN WE NOT ONLY GIVE OUR WORSHIP TO ANOTHER, BUT WE USE THE VERY GIFTS HE HAS GIVEN US IN ORDER TO DO SO!

Not only do we see the holy jealousy and hurt that exists in God's heart as a result of the actions of His people, we also catch a glimpse of His longsuffering and undying love for us, even in the midst of our sin. While He is unwilling (and unable) to compromise His holiness by overlooking our sin, God extends to us every opportunity to recognize our sin, repent of it, and run back to Him. While the Scriptures indicate that God is looking for *voluntary* lovers and will never force us to turn to Him, He does plead with us to embrace truth, and He provides chance after chance for us to do so.

In His attempts to win us back to Himself, it seems that God most often begins by simply placing blessings into our lives that point to Him. After all, we are told in Romans 2:4 that it is the kindness of God that leads us to repentance. However, it is sometimes necessary for God's kindness to take a form that we might not immediately recognize as kindness—that of thornbushes. If it becomes necessary, and it often does, God will take us to the depths of suffering so that we have no other place to turn except back to Him. This is by no means a sign that God has forsaken us or ceased to love us. On the contrary, the fact is that He loves us so much that He would rather see us suffer for a short time than see us suffer for eternity apart from Him. Even though it hurts, this discipline from the Lord is the ultimate kindness that He can show to our weak hearts.

Let's continue to read through the book of Hosea, looking at verses 2:14-18:

> "But then I will win her back once again. I will lead her into the desert and speak tenderly to her there. I will return her vineyards to her and transform the Valley of Trouble into a gateway of hope. She will give herself to me there, as she did long ago when she was young, when I freed her from her captivity in Egypt. When that day comes," says the Lord, "you will call me 'my husband' instead of 'my master.' O Israel, I will wipe the many names of Baal from your lips, and you will never mention them again. On that day I will make a covenant with all the wild animals and the birds of the sky and the animals that scurry along the ground so they will not harm you. I will remove all weapons of war from the land, all swords and bows, so you can live unafraid in peace and safety" (NLT).

This is the promise of the Lord, that for those who would say yes to Him, He will "transform the Valley of Trouble into a gateway of hope." In no way does this mean that life will suddenly become easy; rather, it is a promise from the Lord that He will be intimately present with us as we face life's challenges. Not only that, but God speaks of a time when we will refer to Him as our husband rather than our master. This refers to a day when our obedience and dedication to the Lord will no longer be duty-based but affection-based. We will no longer obey God and submit to His leadership simply because it is right to do so, but because we are madly in love with the One who has wooed us and called us His own.

What the Lord proclaims over His people in the next two verses has quickly become one of my favorite passages of Scripture: "'I will make you my wife forever, showing you righteousness and justice, unfailing love and compassion. I will be faithful to you and make you mine, and you will finally know me as the Lord'" (Hosea 2:19-20, NLT). These are the wedding vows of the faithful bridegroom to His bride, and they cannot be nullified or broken.

Maybe you have been married and, for whatever reason, it didn't work out. Maybe you heard the "'til death do us part" line before, but somehow, though you are still alive, you've parted ways with the one who promised to love you forever. Even if you have not been married, my guess is that you have been hurt and abandoned by someone you thought would always be around. Whatever the case, God is saying, "I understand that you have been hurt, and I understand that people have turned their backs on you, but I want to make you mine *forever*. Not only that, but I want our relationship to be based on righteousness, justice, unfailing love, and compassion. I want you to know me!" Righteousness. Justice. Unfailing love. Compassion. Knowing fully, and being fully known. Forever.

Let's move on in our examination of Hosea's crazy encounter with the Lord. As if it weren't enough that God asked Hosea to find and marry Gomer, when Gomer runs away from Hosea, God tells the prophet that He wants him to go and find her once again: "Then the Lord said to me, 'Go and love your wife again, even though she commits adultery with another lover. This will illustrate that the Lord still loves Israel, even though the people have turned to other gods and love to worship them.' So I bought her back for fifteen pieces of silver and five bushels of barley and a measure of wine" (Hosea 3:1-2).

Let's try to identify with Hosea and his dilemma once again. He is told by God that he is to marry a prostitute named Gomer. He does what he is told, and even though he takes Gomer into his home and loves her, she chooses to return to her former lifestyle. I'm not sure why she leaves. Maybe it is because she has no idea what it looks like to love only one man. Perhaps she has been hurt so badly that she no longer has the emotional capacity to love at all. It's difficult to read this account and not feel at least some level of compassion for Gomer, but my heart hurts for Hosea as well. He has been faithful to God's commands, and according to the passage of Scripture we read, he legitimately loved Gomer. Yet she leaves. If I am Hosea, I'm embarrassed to admit that the story probably ends right here (if it ever gets to this point). However, Hosea is faithful to listen and obey.

God tells Hosea that He wants him to go and get her. Again. Not only is Hosea to go and get her again, he is also to love her. Again. And to make the situation even more difficult to swallow, Hosea must pay a price in order to get Gomer back. He must sacrifice something to reacquire the one who has shunned his love and offering of a better way of life. Is this situation sounding somewhat familiar to you? It should. This is an incredible foreshadowing of the price Jesus would pay to buy back His creation from the curse brought about by our sin.

More Than Forgiveness

Please understand that although the death and resurrection of Jesus makes the forgiveness of God available to all who will accept it, God wants so much more than just to forgive us—His desire is to *marry* us and have us share in ruling His kingdom!

Although most of us have a very difficult time accepting it, God looks at each of us in the midst of our weakness and brokenness and says, "I want you!"

Most of us respond to His offering of love by saying, "I would love to go with You. I would love to dance this dance You are inviting me into. However, there's one problem—I'm all messed up, and I don't think I can ever be any better!" The Lord responds tenderly: "You're right! In your strength you can't be any better, but I am faithful. I died

> GOD WANTS SO MUCH MORE THAN JUST TO FORGIVE US—HIS DESIRE IS TO *MARRY* US AND HAVE US SHARE IN RULING HIS KINGDOM!

for you in the midst of your sin, and I will forgive you and transform you if you will just come after me with all of your heart. Furthermore, beyond simply desiring you, I want to marry you and have an active intimacy with you. My desire is that when I speak, your heart is moved, and when you speak, my heart is moved!"

God does not forgive us so we can spend eternity hanging out in some distant corner of Heaven. Honestly, if that were all there was, that would still be more than we deserve. Let's face it—it would certainly beat the alternative! However, God's desire is to bring us near His heart, to a place even the angels cannot comprehend. It's as if God has set up some sort of boundary line that only His bride, His church, can cross and come near to Him. When we read in the Scriptures of how the angels address God, it is always in terms and titles related to His grandeur. They sing, "Holy, holy, holy is the Lord God Almighty." We too must recognize and celebrate God's omnipotence, so we join with the angels in their song. However, Jesus made it clear to us in His model prayer that when children of God address Him, we are able to call Him "our Father." Again, this is not to say that we should ignore

God's majesty—only that we view God in the same way the angels do, plus we can experience incredible intimacy with Him. What an amazing truth that the Uncreated One, who is well aware of our shortcomings, wants us near Him!

The Personality of the Pursuer

Now that we know that God desires to have an intimate relationship with us, and that He is relentless in His pursuit of our hearts, the thought that naturally arises is: *This sounds too good to be true. Why would God possibly want anything to do with me, let alone marry me?* We received a beautiful glimpse into the heart of the Bridegroom when we examined His wedding vows from Hosea 2:19-20, yet what most of us need to know is how we relate to Him in the midst of our weakness. Surely those vows are only for those who are consistent in their faithfulness and obedience, right? But what about those of us who still find ourselves trying and perpetually coming up short? How does God relate to *us*? The mistake that most of us make in trying to answer this question is to look at ourselves and try to find some good, redeeming quality that could possibly make God like us. However, the Scriptures are clear that there is absolutely no good thing in our flesh. The answer is found only in examining the personality and heart of the One who pursues us.

The first truth we must know is that God is a God of compassion, One who is tender with us in our weaknesses if we are sincere and repentant. To illustrate this point, let's look at a familiar story that Jesus shared with the tax collectors and other "sinners" of His day.

> A man had two sons. The younger son told his father, "I want my share of your estate now before you die." So his father agreed to divide his wealth between his sons.
>
> A few days later this younger son packed all his

belongings and moved to a distant land, and there he wasted all his money in wild living. About the time his money ran out, a great famine swept over the land, and he began to starve. He persuaded a local farmer to hire him, and the man sent him into his fields to feed the pigs. The young man became so hungry that even the pods he was feeding the pigs looked good to him. But no one gave him anything.

When he finally came to his senses, he said to himself, "At home even the hired servants have food enough to spare, and here I am dying of hunger! I will go home to my father and say, 'Father, I have sinned against both heaven and you, and I am no longer worthy of being called your son. Please take me on as a hired servant.'" So he returned home to his father. And while he was still a long way off, his father saw him coming. Filled with love and compassion, he ran to his son, embraced him, and kissed him. His son said to him, "Father, I have sinned against both heaven and you, and I am no longer worthy of being called your son."

But his father said to the servants, "Quick! Bring the finest robe in the house and put it on him. Get a ring for his finger and sandals for his feet. And kill the calf we have been fattening. We must celebrate with a feast, for this son of mine was dead and has now returned to life. He was lost, but now he is found" (Luke 15:11-24, NLT).

As the father looked out and saw his son, in all of his failures and shortcomings, heading up the hill toward home, Jesus tells us that the father was filled with love and compassion for his son. I am sure he could see his son's complete brokenness and penitence, and when he looked out at him he couldn't wait to take the boy in his arms and embrace him.

What's more, Jesus tells us that the father jumped up from the porch and ran out to meet his son. In the culture in which Jesus was relating this parable, wealthy men did not run—

anywhere! This would have been viewed as completely undignified by anyone who might have seen what was taking place. I don't think it is any accident that Jesus tells us that the father did not walk, but ran, to meet his returning son. The father did not force the son to come home, but he was overcome with joy when the boy made the choice to humbly return. When the son starts in by saying, "Dad, stop and let me tell you how bad I am," the father cuts him off and reminds him of his position as a son. God does require repentance to receive His tenderness—we can't live in darkness and compromise and expect God to simply look the other way—but He is compassionate and quick to forgive those who turn from their sin and run to Him.

Not only is God full of compassion and tenderness, He is a God with a happy heart. His heart is marked by overflowing gladness! Most people assume that God is mostly either mad or sad, especially when He thinks about people. In our heart of hearts we hear God saying, "Come to me, all of you who are weary and carry heavy burdens (Matthew 11:28a, NLT) . . . I'm really angry with you, but I guess you can come anyway." Or maybe we think that God is completely disappointed and can hardly stand us, but because He is God, He is just doing the best that He can to "hang in there" and put up with us. However, the truth is that God is not mostly mad or sad, He is mostly glad, especially when He thinks about His bride!

Zephaniah 3:17 tells us, "'The Lord your God in your midst, the Mighty One, will save; He will rejoice over you with gladness, He will quiet you with His love, He will rejoice over you with singing.'" These words are not spoken to a fully mature church, but to a people known for consistently missing the mark. It is so refreshing to know that God actually enjoys you now, that He actually likes you today! It is not as though God despises us through the process of sanctification, and that once we have "arrived" He finally likes us. He enjoys us throughout the process as well.

Now it is important to realize that God is not always glad. He does get both angry and grieved, but He is *mostly* glad. God is grieved when we compromise and don't immediately repent, and if we continue to rebel against Him, then His grief eventually turns to anger.

THERE IS A VAST DIFFERENCE BETWEEN REBELLION AND IMMATURITY.

However, what many of us don't realize is that there is a vast difference between rebellion and immaturity. Rebellion says, "God, I think my way is better than yours, and even though you have called my behavior 'sin,' I am determined to do what I think is best." Immaturity, on the other hand, says, "God, I want so badly to be pleasing to you, but I have messed it up again! I agree with you that what I have done is wrong, and my heart is broken over it. Lord, thank you for your forgiveness, and please give me the grace to quit falling into this mess!" Do you see the difference? It is obvious when the two scenarios are neatly compared side by side in a book like this, but sometimes it is a little more difficult to make the distinction while caught up in the whirlwinds of life. That is why we must continually examine our hearts to determine if we are relating to the Lord out of immaturity or rebellion.

While immaturity does not excuse our behavior, we can be certain that God still likes us and is pleased with our hearts, even though our actions may grieve Him deeply. When we understand and feel God's gladness over our lives, we are empowered to run to Him instead of away from Him when we fall short. A child who does not believe his father loves him will run and hide when he falls short. Conversely, a child who understands that her father truly loves her will always run to him when she stumbles. That is God's desire for His children as well.

Finally, our God is a God with fiery affection and desire.

He really likes you, and He will do whatever He can to win you to Himself. While He will never violate our free will in this area, God will do whatever it takes, within self-imposed limitations, to remove everything in our lives that hinders love. At times, His approach may take the form of *tough love.* Other times, although He promises to never actually leave us or forsake us, His jealous love causes Him to temporarily withdraw any awareness or feeling of His presence so that we are able to fully realize the barrier we are constructing through compromise and lack of repentance. I can tell you firsthand: this one hurts. A lot.

Some time ago, my wife, Carey, and I went through a pretty challenging period in which neither of us were hearing the voice of the Lord clearly. Scratch that. We weren't hearing Him at all. In fact, my heart got so dry at one point that I really began to question whether God was even real, and I was convinced that even if He was, He must not have cared much about being involved in my life. One morning, as we were sitting in a church service, I noticed Carey was crying, which is by no means a regular occurrence. When I leaned over to ask her what was wrong, she whispered through her tears, "I feel like He doesn't even *want* to meet with me anymore." While I had felt the same way for some time, to hear her say the words completely broke me, and as we entered into a time of singing, I unloaded on the Lord. "God, it kills me to hear her talk like that! Why won't you say something? Anything!" As clear as day, I heard Him say in my spirit, "Why doesn't it break your heart that I am saddened when *you* don't want to meet with *me*?"

While His words were kind and in no way condemnatory, what He said caught me completely off guard. To begin with, it was the first time in quite a while that I had heard the Lord speak. Moreover, I realized at that moment that I had never really thought about the Lord's being saddened by my absence.

Well, technically, I guess I had thought about it, because I had heard some teaching on the subject that I remember thinking was pretty cool. In fact, I had memorized and recited it a few times when speaking to various groups, but it quickly became obvious that I didn't really believe it.

To think that God really did miss our times together completely tore me up inside. He has thousands upon thousands upon thousands of followers, yet when I neglect Him, He notices. That afternoon, the reality of God's passionate desire for me became a reality where it had always been merely theoretical. Though I had "known" God for some time, I now knew Him in a way that completely unlocked my heart and freed me to pursue Him without apathy or compromise.

If you are not a follower of Jesus, He wants so badly for you to know that He loves and desires you. He desires a relationship with you so much that He was willing to become a man and die in order to redeem your soul. For those of us who have said yes to Jesus, He longs for us to understand and walk in His extravagant love for us. His heart is ravished with love for us, and He wants so badly to see us begin to live like a bride that is preparing for a wedding with the King—after all, that is what eternity is all about!

Chapter Two

COMMANDED AND EMPOWERED TO LOVE

"Define yourself radically as one beloved by God.
This is the true self. Every other identity is illusion."

–Brennan Manning, *Abba's Child: The Cry of the
Heart for Intimate Belonging*[3]

When I first came into the kingdom of God as a high school student in 1993, I was handed a brand-new paperback Bible and told that in order to really get to know the God who had saved me, I needed to read and somehow comprehend all of the information contained within that intimidating book. I had always been a really good student, and I prided myself on my ability to read and regurgitate information during a test, so I gladly accepted what I considered to be a worthy challenge.

---

[3] Brennan Manning, *Abba's Child: The Cry of the Heart for Intimate Belonging* (Colorado Springs: NavPress, 1994), 42.

I was not given a great deal of specific direction, so I did the only thing I knew to do and started reading at the beginning. Genesis. "In the beginning . . . . " It seemed to make perfect sense that if I wanted to understand the story, this was the place to start.

As I read through the account of creation, I was awed and amazed by the power and creativity of God. I wept as I was introduced to the fall of mankind in the garden. I even experienced some feelings of anger toward Adam and Eve for completely blowing it with God and thrusting us headlong into the chaos we experience today (although I have realized through the years that I would have undoubtedly responded much like they did). I was inspired by the recounting of the life of Abraham, who left everything he owned and knew to partner with God in establishing a new people who would be set apart for the Lord. And then there was Moses, a stuttering failure in the eyes of his own people, who faithfully led the people of God out of Egyptian captivity and started them on their journey to the Promised Land.

Then I hit the proverbial brick wall. Based upon the numerous stories I have heard through the years, it is the same impasse that countless others have encountered in their attempts to read the Scriptures cover to cover: the book of Leviticus. As I read through the Law that God gave the Israelites while having no real knowledge of the heart of the One who had given that Law, I got bogged down and, quite frankly, became bored with what I was reading. I couldn't make myself press through, and I wound up feeling like a complete failure. Honestly, I was also a little disgusted . . . and maybe a bit angry as well. Suddenly, God seemed like an overly emotional, extremist, overbearing tyrant. I remember walking away and never even picking up the Bible for a fairly significant amount of time. After a few months passed, I resolved to give it one more try, thinking that if I started at the beginning once again, I could establish

IMAGINE THE RELIEF I FELT WHEN I BEGAN TO READ OF THIS MAN NAMED JESUS, WHO WAS FULL OF COMPASSION, MERCY, AND GRACE!

enough momentum to carry me through Leviticus and into what was sure to follow. Eventually I gave up counting how many times I attempted and failed with this process and just abandoned the Old Testament altogether, choosing instead to begin anew in the New Testament and the Gospel of Matthew.

Imagine the relief I felt when I began to read of this man named Jesus, who was full of compassion, mercy, and grace! While I knew that the Scriptures said He was the Son of God, I could not begin to reconcile how such a man could possibly be the son of such a strict and rule-absorbed slave driver as the God of the Old Testament. Yet the Bible tells us that Jesus is "the radiance of God's glory and the *exact representation* of his being" (Hebrews 1:3). To put it mildly, after my experiences in attempting to digest the Old Testament, I was dumbfounded and frustrated beyond words.

Hanging the Law and the Prophets

One afternoon as I was reading through Matthew, God graciously began to shine a light on the truth of His character and the heart behind the Law He had given Moses. As Jesus was being challenged by the religious leaders of His day, He made a profound statement that provides us the lens through which the entire Old Testament is to be read and understood: "Hearing that Jesus had silenced the Sadducees, the Pharisees got together. One of them, an expert in the law, tested him with this question: 'Teacher, which is the greatest commandment in the Law?' Jesus replied: 'Love the Lord your God with all your heart and with all your soul and with all your mind.

This is the first and greatest commandment. And the second is like it: Love your neighbor as yourself. *All the Law and Prophets hang on these two commandments*" (Matthew 22:34-40, NIV, emphasis mine).

Who would have thought? All the Law and the Prophets boiled down to two simple commandments.

Understanding what Jesus is saying here allows for a completely different reading of the Old Testament, especially for those of us in Western culture. When I originally read through the Law of Moses, I understood the commandments of God as something I was to try with all of my might to achieve, and if I were somehow able to fulfill them, God would receive me as His own. Then, and only then, would God be proud enough to accept me as His child. To me, many of the commandments in the Law seemed either harsh or completely random—there was no way I could even remember all of them, let alone keep them! And if I failed, well, then I received the harsh judgments that were so often proclaimed by the Old Testament prophets. For the longest time, my performance-driven mindset killed my desire to read major sections of Scripture since I knew I was bound to fail and feel condemned when I did.

As I gained understanding regarding God's desire to foster a love relationship with me, even the most difficult sections of the Law and the most unpalatable prophets began to reveal an entirely new dimension of God's heart. While there are still some obscure commandments in the Law that I must admit I don't understand completely, and while the words of many of the prophets still seem exceptionally harsh, my heart rejoices to know that they can all be boiled down to two primary points: loving God and loving others. The primary commandments given to us are to set our hearts on falling more in love with Jesus, and to learn to love others out of the overflow that comes from experiencing intimacy with His heart. Every other purpose and calling under Heaven "hangs" on these two heart commitments.

In trying to understand the fullness of what Jesus is saying here, it helps me to think of the two great commandments as the skeleton on which the muscles, flesh, and skin—the commandments of the Law and the wisdom of the prophets—"hang." Without the skeleton, the rest is nothing more than a big pile of mush. In effect, Jesus is saying there is nothing in the history and purpose of the nation of Israel that is not firmly founded in the commandments to love God and love others. Love is what was on God's mind when He called Israel to be His people and set them apart as a consecrated nation. That purpose has not changed. In fact, love is what was on God's mind when He created the New Jerusalem, in which those who have said yes to Jesus will spend eternity in intimate fellowship with the Father.

> THE ONE WHO GIVES THE COMMANDMENTS IS THE SAME ONE WHO EMPOWERS US TO KEEP THEM, SO THERE IS HOPE FOR US YET!

All the purposes and plans of God spring forth from the commandments to love. Furthermore, through the death and resurrection of Jesus, the Holy Spirit has been made available as the source of power through which all of this takes place! The One who gives the commandments is the same One who empowers us to keep them, so there is hope for us yet!

Equally Yoked in Love

God's ultimate eternal purpose for creation is to provide a bride who will be equally yoked in love to Jesus. His desire is to provide a family of faithful children for Himself and an eternal companion for His Son, a bride whom He fully possesses in love. This is a promise that the Father has made to the Son, and nothing will stop Him from carrying it to completion: "I [the Father] will give You [Jesus] the nations for Your inheritance, and the ends of the earth for Your possession" (Psalm 2:8). Not only has the Father promised this inheritance to the Son, the Son has come into agreement with the Father in prayer regarding this promise: "And I have declared to them Your name, and will declare it, that the love with which You loved Me may be in them" (John 17:26). Jesus asks the Father that the same love with which the Father loves the Son would be the love with which the bride loves the Son. This is a prayer from God, the Son, to God, the Father. It *must* be answered! It is impossible for the Son to pray amiss or outside of the Father's will. We *will* love Jesus the same way the Father does!

So what does it look like for us to love Jesus in this way? What does it mean for the bride to be "equally yoked" to Jesus in love? In short, God wants us to be captivated by His Son and to voluntarily love Him with all that we are, because He loves us with all that He is. The great news is that He will supernaturally empower us to love Him in this way. One of the foundational premises of Scripture is that it takes God to love God—we *cannot* love Him apart from His Spirit working within us. The anointing to receive and return God's love is the greatest gift that is imparted by the Holy Spirit to any disciple of Jesus: "[T]he love of God has been poured out in our hearts by the Holy Spirit who was given to us" (Romans 5:5).

God is looking for so much more than that we just "grit our teeth" and do the best we can to obey and love Him. Sure, there will come a day when God will cause all of creation to obey Jesus: "Therefore God exalted him to the highest place and gave him the name that is above every name, that at the name of Jesus every knee should bow, in heaven and on earth and under the earth, and every tongue acknowledge that Jesus Christ is Lord, to the glory of God the Father" (Philippians 2:9-

11, NIV). However, the Father's purpose is to raise up a bride who will respond to Jesus in voluntary love, and through the working of that love in her heart, become prepared to reign with Jesus for eternity.

Rest assured, the first commandment will be restored to first place in the church before Jesus returns: "For the marriage of the Lamb has come, and His wife has made herself ready" (Revelation 19:7). We "make ourselves ready" by realigning our lives and ministries to make the first commandment first in priority. He will not force us into a relationship, but when we open our hearts in voluntary love and abandonment, setting our hearts to know and love Him, He so graciously "washes us with the water of the Word" (Ephesians 5:26). Through His Word He reveals His heart to us, and in experiencing Him there we are empowered to love in return.

It Is What He Says It Is

Considering all this talk of voluntarily loving Jesus with all that is within us, maybe it is worth taking a little time to put some definition to the word *love*. Of all the words in the English language, I would argue that this word is probably the most overused, and this *over*use has resulted in its *mis*use and its depth of meaning being lost in translation.

When I married Carey, I made an oath in front of God, our families, and our friends to love her through thick and thin. Looking back, at that time I honestly had no idea what I was promising. (Although I would—and do—make the same promise again today.) While our relationship had been tested during the time leading up to our wedding day, we had no idea of the challenges that were to come. Trying to blend two lives into one is difficult and should never be taken lightly. We had a strong friendship and an emotional connection that I cherished, but we were forced to learn very early on in our marriage that love entails so much more than feelings.

While passion is certainly an important element of what is entailed in loving someone or something, love, at its core, is a commitment that endures even when strong emotions fade. I would compare "love" based purely on passion to a beach house that is built directly on the sand—while the view may be wonderful, when the winds of adversity blow, that house is sure to come crashing down. However, if an effort is made to build a deep concrete foundation, not only is there a wonderful view, the house structure is more likely to stand.

Let's observe how the Apostle Paul defines love in 1 Corinthians 13:4-8: "Love suffers long and is kind; love does not envy; love does not parade itself, is not puffed up; does not behave rudely, does not seek its own, is not provoked, thinks no evil; does not rejoice in iniquity, but rejoices in the truth; bears all things, believes all things, hopes all things, endures all things. Love never fails."

Did you notice all of the "passion" phrases that Paul uses in defining love? If so, go back and read the passage again, because such words simply do not exist in Paul's definition. Love, in Paul's mind, is based primarily on character and commitment rather than how we may or may not feel on a given day.

Let's take the discussion a step further. I will make the statement that I love my wife with everything that is in me, and that statement is true. However, I have also been known to speak of my "love" for Asian cuisine from time to time. Really? I desire with all my heart to be patient and kind to my wife, but fried rice and egg rolls don't really stir up those same longings. Yet the best word I can come up with to describe the emotional response I feel when presented with a plate of fresh sushi is "love." How foolish and irresponsible is it that we use the same word to speak of our dinner that we use to speak of the sacred institution of marriage?

Reducing the significance and implications associated with the word *love* has allowed us to apply it easily when speaking of the emotions we might have toward God. During my twenty or so years in various forms of ministry to youth, I have lost count of the number of teenagers who have spoken to me of their "love" for God while obviously having no experiential knowledge of Him whatsoever. This became even clearer to me with the advent of social networking sites such as Twitter and Facebook. Numerous times I have seen teenagers who proclaim their "love" for Jesus in their "About Me" section—and then brag of their sexual exploits and alcohol/drug abuse in their posts. While I understand and agree that perfection is not a prerequisite for loving God (thankfully!), if we truly love Him, does it make sense to brag about doing the very things that break His heart? If we hurt another person we truly love, we expect that we would feel strong remorse and regret. However, we have come to believe that we can "love" God while blowing off His feelings and standards regarding our behavior. And I am not just picking on teenagers: most of us have likely been guilty, at least from time to time, of offering lip service that is not consistent with our lifestyle.

In John 14:15-24, Jesus defines love for God as being deeply rooted in a spirit of obedience: "If you love Me, keep My commandments. . . . He who has My commandments and keeps them, it is he who loves Me. . . . If anyone loves Me, he will keep My word . . . He who does not love Me does not keep My words." According to Jesus, there is no such thing as loving God without seeking to obey His Word. This is not to say that we must get it right every time; only that we must set our hearts to obey, making every effort to partner with the Holy Spirit as He works on making our hearts submissive to God. At the same time, true love requires that heart responses eventually be accompanied by follow-through. We must be careful not to reduce love for Jesus to rhetoric about being radically devoted or "sold out" without any real expression of love in our lives that is defined according to God's terms. While loving God is certainly more than *just* obeying His commandments, the two cannot be separated.

Denying our lustful desires and submitting our will to the Lord in the midst of great temptation is one of the primary theaters God has chosen for us in which we are to express our love to Him. Each of us has a different struggle according to our personality and circumstances; therefore, we each have a different assignment through which we offer our gift of love to God. Whatever that specific assignment looks like, Jesus takes it personally when we resist sin because of love. Consider this: it is only in this short life, in this age, that we have the opportunity to glorify God by growing in love and faithfulness while enduring hardship, pain, pressure, and temptation. After death or His return to earth, this great opportunity ceases. Let's not waste this limited time opportunity!

CONSIDER THIS: IT IS ONLY IN THIS SHORT LIFE, IN THIS AGE, THAT WE HAVE THE OPPORTUNITY TO GLORIFY GOD BY GROWING IN LOVE AND FAITHFULNESS WHILE ENDURING HARDSHIP, PAIN, PRESSURE, AND TEMPTATION. AFTER DEATH OR HIS RETURN TO EARTH, THIS GREAT OPPORTUNITY CEASES.

Loving God requires so much more than simply singing to Him or having sentimental feelings about a god that we make in our own image. We must love God on God's terms, and God is not a humanistic hippie. A core issue at the end of this age will be whether we have loved God according to His definition or according to the definition of a culture that seeks to love without obedience and adherence to God's Word. Jesus longs for a love from His bride that is marked by submission to His will and an overarching desire to bring Him glory on earth. While this may sound unacceptable and overbearing in a culture that values "individualism" and "freedom," we must understand that true freedom is only found in submitting to His leadership—and it is the only love that God receives as genuine. When we realize that all of His commandments are related to love—He commands us to stay near His heart, to seek His face, to choose love over lust, to pursue eternal rewards rather than temporal ones, to be vessels of love to others through service—we will fully comprehend what it means to truly walk in freedom.

First Things First

Now that we have a working definition of *love* according to the Word of God, let's dig a little deeper into Jesus' words in Matthew 22:37-38: "Love the Lord your God with all your heart and with all your soul and with all your mind. This is the first and greatest commandment" (NIV).

The reason God has said that loving Him is the "first commandment" is because it takes precedence over everything else in the life of a disciple. While God has definite, individual plans and desires for each one of us, at the top of His priority list for *all* of us is that we love Him with everything that we are. Most of us who have at some point said yes to Jesus' leadership in our lives have then spent significant time and energy repeatedly asking, "What is God's will for my life?" In most cases, what we are really asking is, "What is my ministry assignment while I am here on earth?" While this is a valid question to ask, we must at the same time realize that our primary assignment in the will of God is to grow in love.

In fact, it is a commandment!

Notice that Jesus did not call the commandment to love

God with all that is in us the "first option" or "a really good idea." The fact is that Jesus is resolute when it comes to having *all* of who we are; He desires a bride without spot or wrinkle. While we may measure success in life based on money, wisdom, fame, and influence, Jesus' criteria are drastically different. The question by which God will judge our lives at the end of the age is: *Did you learn to love?* He wants to awaken our spirits to reveal and impart His love to us. Everything that God does, He does first and foremost for love.

THE QUESTION BY WHICH GOD WILL JUDGE OUR LIVES AT THE END OF THE AGE IS: *DID YOU LEARN TO LOVE?*

Biblical Christianity is not primarily about acting or living in a certain way or even about giving our lives in service to others. While it is true that people who experience the work of the Holy Spirit in their hearts will exhibit the fruits of righteousness and service, true Christianity is concerned primarily with an ongoing encounter of love with a Person. Possessing fierce dedication and making radical choices for righteousness will not keep us steady unless we learn to walk in love with that Person. It is not enough to be part of a mission or to have a vision to change a city or a nation. The labor of the vision will make us weary without the small but consistent stirring of love by the Holy Spirit in our hearts. Effective ministry, and more importantly, a life that is pleasing to the Father, begins in the place of intimacy with His heart.

But Jesus not only calls loving God the "first commandment," He also calls it the "greatest commandment." Of all the commandments in the Law, why would God so elevate this one? I believe it is because loving God has the greatest impact on His heart, our hearts, and the hearts of those with whom we come in contact. Loving Him is our greatest calling; it is what Jesus esteems as the greatest way to live, and it is how

He measures the quality of our ministry. It is the only thing we can do that is guaranteed to have fruit that will last for eternity.

While impacting people is very important, our *greatest* calling is to impact God's heart. If we are consistently encountering God in the place of intimacy, we cannot help but impact those around us. At the same time, if we call others to embrace and to live the "greatest commandment," we help them set paths that will result in their greatest fulfillment and impact in the kingdom. While loving God is a great and glorious end in itself, it cannot help but overflow into loving ourselves and others, both believers and unbelievers.

So if our greatest calling is to impact the heart of God through our wholehearted love for Him, the question we must be able to answer is: How do I express my love for God in a way that truly moves Him? As we discussed earlier, we move His heart by even the smallest intention of our heart to obey. Each time we repent of compromise, it moves Him. We move His heart by simply sitting before him like Mary of Bethany (Luke 10:38-42; more on this later) or performing small acts of service for others that are motivated by our love for Him rather than our desire for recognition and accolades (Matthew 10:42). We cannot allow ourselves to become captivated by persuading more people to receive our ministry or to listen to us preach, sing, etc. God is not impressed with or moved by our outward ministry. He is only moved by the hidden activities of our heart.

God has placed in each of us a desire to be great. Every individual has within him or her the desire to make a lasting impact on the world in which he or she lives. While we must consistently embrace humility and servanthood, the desire for greatness is not something that we can or should repent of. God has placed it in our heart, and it is therefore not a sin to have such a desire. Where we often miss the mark is in the way we go about fulfilling this desire. You can be one of the greatest people in history simply by living in obedience to and in deep love for God. You will more than likely not be one of the most famous, but you can be one of the greatest: "Whoever therefore breaks one of the least of these commandments, and teaches men so, shall be called least in the kingdom of heaven; but whoever does and teaches them, he shall be called great in the kingdom of heaven" (Matthew 5:19).

While we search for satisfaction and significance in so many different places, our greatest satisfaction and significance is found in knowing and feeling God's love, loving Him in return, and loving others out of the overflow in our hearts. Our "inner man" is strengthened (Ephesians 3:16) as we live out affection-based obedience that flows from experiencing Jesus' affection and responding in love. This is the most consistent form of obedience simply because a person who is lovesick is willing to endure anything for love. That is precisely why Satan's priority is to distract us from cultivating wholehearted love and devotion to Jesus: "But I am afraid that, as the serpent deceived Eve by his craftiness, your minds will be led astray from the simplicity and purity of devotion to Christ" (2 Corinthians 11:3, NASB). Setting our hearts to live as extravagant lovers of God makes us less susceptible to compromise and enables us to avoid becoming trapped in bitterness when we are mistreated and persecuted.

OH, THAT WE WOULD LEARN TO BE BOLD ENOUGH TO ASK, "WHAT IS THE MOST THAT GOD WILL EMPOWER ME TO GIVE TO HIM?"

In short, the anointing to love God is our greatest possession. As with all of His commandments, the commandment to love comes with the promise of His supernatural enabling to obey. However, love does not automatically grow—we must actively cultivate extravagant devotion to Jesus. This takes time and effort on our part, and if we do not intentionally cultivate the work of the Holy Spirit in our life, our heart will eventually grow cold. Oh, that we would learn to be bold enough to ask, "What is the most that God will empower me to give to Him?" rather than being content with meeting the "minimum requirements" for salvation!

The reward of love is found in possessing the power to love. In other words, as we love Him, we are empowered to love Him more. As we are empowered to love Him more, sin and compromise are much less appealing. Each time we are tempted to give up on our pursuit of knowing God, the obstacle that stands in our way is that we are madly in love with Him. We begin to identify ourselves primarily as lovers of God who struggle with sin rather than as sinners who struggle to love God. We no longer define ourselves by our accomplishments, but our spiritual identity can be summarized in this way: "I am loved by God, and I am a lover of God. Therefore, I am successful." Wow! This really *is* a great commandment!

Chapter Three

DEFINING WHOLEHEARTED LOVE: FOUR STAGES AND SPHERES

"Do you know that nothing you do in this
life will ever matter, unless it is about loving God
and loving the people He has made?"

– Francis Chan, *Crazy Love: Overwhelmed
by a Relentless God*[4]

In our pursuit of becoming wholehearted lovers of God, it might help to start with a clear definition of exactly what "wholehearted love" looks like. As we discussed in the last chapter, we must love God according to His definition, which requires setting our hearts to obey His commandments. However, Jesus tells us that His primary commandments are that we love Him and love others. If we combine the texts of

---

[4] Francis Chan, *Crazy Love: Overwhelmed by a Relentless God* (Colorado Springs: David C. Cook, 2013), 97.

John 14:15-24 ("If you love me, keep my commandments") and Matthew 22:34-40 ("Love the Lord your God"), in effect, what Jesus is telling us is, "If you love me . . . love me." Let's dig a little deeper to determine exactly what He is saying here.

We'll begin by examining the God-ordained process by which we become wholehearted lovers of Jesus. God has established a series of stages through which our hearts are transformed, and as with most things, if we try to reverse the steps or shortcut His process, our desired results will not be realized. We will examine each of the stages in this progression in more detail in this chapter, but for now, here's a quick summary:

1. **We receive love from God.**

2. **We give love back to God.**

3. **We are empowered to love ourselves.**

4. **We love others out of the overflow.**

Again, let me be clear: following this progression is the *only* way we will ever truly love God according to His definition. However, it is important to make a few clarifications. First, these are not steps that we move through in the sense of perfecting one in order to "move on" to the next. We don't ever want to move on from receiving love from God or from loving Him in return in order to love ourselves or other people. That simply doesn't make any sense. Instead, we should think of these stages as building upon one another; each stage is the foundation for the ones that follow. Also, we don't wait until we have "perfected" stages one, two, and three before we get to stage four. If we do, we will never get past the first stage! His love for us is boundless, and we cannot fully comprehend it! We can live in each stage simultaneously, but our success in the latter stages is dependent on how well the earlier stages have been established in our lives.

The main point we must understand is that we cannot skip any steps in this progression, and we cannot reverse the order. It is impossible for us to truly love God until we have received love from Him. Until we are empowered to love God, we cannot love ourselves in a healthy way. And until we learn to love ourselves, we cannot truly love those around us. We must enter the progression at the only place that makes sense: the beginning. The mistake that many of us make is that we reverse the order and attempt to earn God's love by how we treat others. Here are the phases by which many of us mistakenly approach our walk with God:

1. We attempt to love others by serving them in some way.

2. We feel good about ourselves because of what we have done for others.

3. We convince ourselves that what we have done for others is to be received by God as love toward Him.

4. We believe that God must love us in return because of what we have done.

Following this reversed progression will result in burnout and does not allow us to experience God in a meaningful way. Also, this way of thinking completely violates one of the foundational truths of the Gospel, which is that we receive God's love and salvation by grace alone, not by our works. Our good works are to be the result of our experiencing the transforming power of His love, not an attempt at earning it. Pursuing the latter is nothing short of the dreaded "L" word: legalism. Usually this word is thrown around to dissuade those who are pursuing an uncompromising, righteous lifestyle. However, there is nothing at all legalistic about passionately going after good works and holy living. The problem arises when we begin to believe that our good works earn us anything from God. God certainly does receive righteous choices and acts of kindness toward others as offerings of love to Himself (Matthew 25:32-40), but His ultimate desire is that we do our acts of service out of a position of intimate partnership with His Spirit.

So if basing our life in God purely on service to and love for others can easily lead to legalism, what if we enter the progression at one of the other stages? For example, what if we begin at stage 3, loving ourselves? As you read this, you are probably thinking it sounds silly to begin your pursuit of a passionate relationship with Jesus by focusing on loving yourself more (and it is!), but this seems to be a trend that is becoming more prevalent with each passing day, at least in Western culture. Many of the most popular voices in the Western church have built quite a following by promoting a self-help/self-love approach to sharing the gospel. While I truly believe many who take this approach mean well, I can't begin to understand the motivation behind it. My best guess is there is an underlying belief that if people are made to feel good about themselves and their potential, this will unlock their heart to hear truths about God's love that they could not otherwise receive. On the surface, this sounds like solid methodology, but there are a couple of problems worth noting.

First, if we build our relationship with God on a foundation of self-love, what happens when we fail in a big, obvious, undeniable way? What happens when we have been told over and over again how gifted, talented, beautiful, and good we are, yet we are suddenly faced with the reality that none of our natural abilities, beauty, or morality is enough to carry us through? If we have allowed ourselves to believe, even for a moment, that God's love is somehow based on our own personality, skills, abilities, popularity, or influence, then our foundation cracks and the house comes tumbling down. However, the heart that has learned that it is infinitely valuable simply because it is loved by God is able to arise and move forward, falling deeper in love with God because of His great mercy and grace.

This brings us to the next important point. The foundational beauty of the gospel is that "while we were still sinners, Christ died for us" (Romans 5:8). There is nothing good, lovely, or otherwise appealing about us that does not originate with Him. We need to know that. Completely. While I am not in favor of presenting the gospel in a manner that berates and demeans, it does seem counterproductive to make people feel as good about themselves as possible while sharing with them their great need for a Savior! I don't recall a single instance in Scripture in which Jesus encounters an individual and begins the conversation by telling him how much natural skill, ability, and beauty he possesses. He doesn't try to convince her that her feelings of emptiness are founded in not believing in herself enough to reach her full potential. Instead, Jesus typically uncovers the person's brokenness and sin and presents Himself as the answer. It is as if He knows that people's hearts will be unlocked only as they encounter unconditional love in the midst of their desperate situations.

The last option we have as a starting point, at least in the progression I have outlined here, is to attempt to begin at stage 2 by working up a love for God in our own strength. While the primary focus of this book is on growing in love for God, a foundational principle is that we are completely incapable of doing so, at least in any meaningful, sustainable way, apart from a consistent awareness and experience of His love for us. "We love Him because He first loved us" (1 John 4:19). Otherwise, our love has no foundation. A "love" for God that is not rooted in an experience of the love flowing from His heart is little more than an expression of emotionalism and zeal. It is unsustainable, especially in the face of persecution and difficulty. It will not last.

I can't emphasize strongly enough the importance of

I CAN'T EMPHASIZE STRONGLY ENOUGH THE IMPORTANCE OF BEGINNING AT THE BEGINNING— UNDERSTANDING AND RECEIVING GOD'S LOVE IN THE MIDST OF OUR BROKENNESS AND NEED.

beginning at the beginning—understanding and receiving God's love in the midst of our brokenness and need. Focusing on loving and serving others apart from an awareness of God's love for us and for the ones we are serving can easily lead to legalism. Emphasizing love for ourselves is humanism. Beginning by trying to force our hearts to love God is emotionalism. Each of these "isms" falls far short of God's plan and desire for our lives. Love for God, love for ourselves, and love for others are all beautiful and necessary, but these are all streams that must flow from the river of God's great love for us!

Now let's examine each of these phases in the progression of wholehearted love in more detail.

Stage One: Increased Revelation of God's Supernatural Love

This is so critical that it bears repeating: the only place to start in our progression toward growing in love for God is at the beginning, understanding the incredible love the Father has for us. It is impossible to truly love God without first understanding this reality. There is no getting around it—we must have an increased revelation of the passionate love that Jesus has for His bride. That is the reason for Paul's prayer for the believers in Ephesus (and for all believers):

> I pray that out of his glorious riches he may strengthen you with power through his Spirit in your inner being, so that Christ may dwell in your hearts through faith.

And I pray that you, being rooted and established in love, may have power, together with all the Lord's holy people, to grasp how wide and long and high and deep is the love of Christ, and to know this love that surpasses knowledge—that you may be filled to the measure of all the fullness of God (Ephesians 3:16-19, NIV).

Paul prays that we would be "rooted and established" in our understanding of God's love. It is the foundation, the starting point for everything that follows. It is the truth that equips us to love God in a way that is steady and will stand the test of time and hardship. He also asks that we would understand the fullness of the love of Christ—the width, length, height, and depth. It is difficult to wrap our natural minds around the fact that Jesus loves us with the same intensity with which the Father loves the Son, but Jesus Himself said that is the case: "As the Father loved Me, I also have loved you; abide in My love" (John 15:9). When we understand this truth, it gives us the freedom to stand before God with confidence and boldly proclaim, "He loves me! I am one of His favorites!" When we are able to do this, it frees us to love Him in return. If you are struggling to believe that God truly feels this way about you, pray along with Paul that the Holy Spirit will help you gain experiential knowledge of the Father's love. I am convinced there are few prayers He is more excited to answer!

Stage Two: Receiving the Father's Love for Jesus By the Power of the Holy Spirit

In Jesus' high priestly prayer recorded in John 17, He prays, "I have made you known to them, and will continue to make you known in order that the love you have for me may be in them and that I myself may be in them" (John 17:26, NIV). Jesus is saying that He has revealed the Father to us in fullness, showing us His incredible love in order to set us free to love Him in return. Not only that, but He asks the Father to impart to our hearts *the same love with which the Father loves the Son.* What an incredible request! The anointing to receive God's love and then return it back to Him is the greatest gift the Holy Spirit imparts to our hearts. Paul tells us that "the love of God has been poured out in our hearts by the Holy Spirit" (Romans 5:5). Love for God is a gift that comes to us through the work of the Holy Spirit, and it begins with a revelation of His love for us. In short, it takes God to love God, and He freely gives this love to all who earnestly desire it.

With this in mind, let's continue our conversation regarding loving God on His terms. I stated earlier that those who truly love God will keep His commandments, but we must be aware that there are different "flavors" of obedience. I touched on this briefly in the previous chapter, but I believe it deserves further discussion.

> IT TAKES GOD TO LOVE GOD, AND HE FREELY GIVES THIS LOVE TO ALL WHO EARNESTLY DESIRE IT.

The most basic form of obedience is fear-based obedience, which is obedience that is motivated by the fear of negative consequences. While this is not the strongest form of obedience or the one most desired by God, it is still biblical. Jesus consistently makes mention of the reality of Hell, the ultimate punishment for those who rebel against God and choose to ignore His love and leadership in their lives.

A second form of obedience is duty-based obedience. This speaks of a commitment to obey the Lord even when we do not feel God's presence or have any strong inspiration to do so. This too is a biblical motivation for obedience, as God's Word requires that we obey even when our feelings are contrary to the commandment.

While we will often find ourselves relating to God in the place of fear-based or duty-based obedience, both of which are healthy and biblical, the ultimate form of obedience is affection-based obedience. The reason I refer to this as the *ultimate* form of obedience is that it is the one that will stand the test of time. It is the obedience that flows from experiencing Jesus' great affection for us and then giving it back to Him through the power of the Holy Spirit at work in our hearts. Love for God and the desire to obey will grow in us as we are moved by the truth of His greatness and by the gratitude that comes from seeing the full story related to how He is treating us.

Affection-based obedience is the strongest, deepest, and most consistent form of obedience because a person who is lovesick is willing to endure anything for love. He or she will face any challenge and endure any hardship to experience the freedom and joy that is found in loving wholeheartedly. We were created with a longing to be wholehearted and abandoned, and thus to know the joy of lovesickness. There is nothing more satisfying than having the power to give the deepest affection of our heart to God and to remain loyal in love, regardless of the consequences. We long to possess the power to be abandoned in love instead of being stuck in boredom, passivity, disloyalty, and compromise, all conditions that leave us broken and discontented.

Stage Three: Loving Ourselves in the Grace of God

Jesus tells us that the second greatest commandment is that we love others around us "as *we love ourselves*" (Matthew 22:39). For some of us, this might actually present the most daunting challenge in the entire passage. Actually, the problem for many of us is that we *do* love our neighbor as we love ourselves. We just don't love ourselves very well. Worse yet, we have become OK with that. In fact, for many of us, the idea of loving ourselves might even seem sacrilegious or blasphemous. I think there are a number of reasons for this: we have been told we are worthless by others, we don't understand grace and the reality of how God feels about us (we think we are agreeing with God when we are actually in opposition to Him), or we don't believe our love for God is real (we see ourselves as hopeless hypocrites).

Before we can love our neighbor as ourselves and actually fulfill the commandments of Jesus, we must first learn to love ourselves in the grace of God. I am not talking about loving ourselves in a fleshly or selfish way, but in a way that simply agrees with God—knowing and affirming what we look like to Him and who we are in Christ as His inheritance. This includes valuing and rejoicing in who God made us to be both physically and in our personality, gifts, and talents. We must know who we are in Christ and rejoice in that reality. If we understand, believe, and have a healthy focus on who we are through the prophetic decree of the Lord, and not just on who we are today in our immaturity and weaknesses, we can begin to love ourselves, not just because of who we are, but because of who He is in us and who we will become. If the idea of loving yourself in the grace of God seems foreign, overwhelming, or even heretical to you, take a look at the words of King David in Psalm 139:13-17:

> For you created my inmost being; you knit me together in my mother's womb. I praise you because I am fearfully and wonderfully made; your works are wonderful, I know that full well. My frame was not hidden from you when I was made in the secret place, when I was woven together in the depths of the earth. Your eyes saw my unformed body; all the days ordained for me were written in your book before one of them came to be (NIV).

Do these sound like the words of one who despised himself or did not place a high value on what the Lord had done in creating him? After speaking about God's handiwork in "knitting him together in his mother's womb," David tells the Lord how wonderful His works are! It might make you a little uncomfortable to say the same thing about yourself, but that does not make it any less true. It simply means that you have not learned to love yourself within the grace of God. As God reveals His amazing love to you, and as you are set free and empowered to love Him in return, ask Him to also free you to love yourself in a way that honors Him and reflects His glory to the world.

This seems like a perfect time to address an issue that plagues the body of Christ and keeps us from fully partnering with God in a way that is most effective to the kingdom: envy. If we are honest, most of us would admit that we have at some point wished that we had the gifts, talents, personality, looks, relationships, influence, or resources of another brother or sister in Christ. I know I have, and envy has kept me in bondage and paralyzed me in my partnership with the Lord. Not only that, but it has kept me from fully experiencing the love of God and the freedom that comes with simply being His child. (After all, how could God really love me as much as He loves _____?)

We cannot allow ourselves to secretly (or openly) wish we were someone else, as if God somehow made a mistake in creating us. In fact, to dislike and despise ourselves is actually to call God's leadership into question. That may not be our intent, but if we truly believe we were created by God, then who are we to question or despise what He has made? Indeed, when we choose the path of comparison, we open the door to bitterness, believing that we are insignificant to God or that He favors others over us. This bitterness will cause our hearts to shut down toward God, and it will hinder our ability to receive His love and return love to Him. It is only as we take our eyes off of others and off of our own failures, choosing instead to focus on His grace, that we will truly learn to appreciate God's workmanship and love who He created us to be.

GOD HAS DECLARED THAT YOU HAVE VALUE! AGREE WITH HIM!

God has declared that you have value! Agree with Him! You are not selfish or self-centered in doing so. He created us with value and purpose. He loves His children and doesn't want anyone talking badly about them—including themselves. How much sense does it make to continue to argue with Him? Instead, take your eyes off other people, and your own failures, and focus on the reality of what He says. You just might learn to appreciate what you see!

Stage Four: Loving Others Out of the Overflow

The final phase in the progression toward holy passion is learning to love others well. This is the visible evidence of our love for God. In fact, Jesus tells us in John 13:34-35 that the way the world will know that we are His disciples, that we truly love Him and long to be like Him, is if we love one another. Throughout the book of 1 John (among other places) we are told that we do not truly love God if we do not also love our brothers. This is why Jesus says the second great commandment, to love our neighbor as ourselves, is "like" the first. They are very closely related. It is only in being energized by feeling God's love, loving Him in return, and experiencing the freedom to love ourselves that we are able to consistently and rightly overflow in love for others. At the same time, if we don't love those around us, that is evidence that our relationship with God and our love for Him is lacking.

Before we leave this subject, there are three major truths I would like to point out. We will look at each of these in more detail later, but I think it is important to at least mention them now.

First, "loving others" without the power of God at work in our lives is actually not love at all. While I appreciate secular humanitarian efforts, the only love that truly makes a lasting difference, the only love that has the power to truly set the captive heart free, is the love that proceeds from the heart of the Father. That is why it is critical that our love for others results from an overflow of His love within our own hearts. There is much talk of justice and service to the poor within the church today, and that is a very good thing. God loves justice, and He loves the poor. In fact, He loves them much more than we could ever imagine. But woe to us as the body of Christ if we embrace "justice" and service to *anyone* without first allowing our hearts to be "rooted and grounded in love," whereby we experience a thriving relationship with the source of all true love in the secret places of our hearts.

The second truth is that attempting to love others apart from first loving God is not sustainable. Trust me, I speak from experience. Human zeal will carry us to a certain point, but eventually "burnout" and frustration are inevitable. In fact, one of Satan's primary tactics is to simply wait patiently while we stumble around in our own strength. He does not have to intervene in any way; he knows we will fail. That failure typically leads to a rift in our relationship with God as we blame Him for not coming through for us in a situation He was never committed to in the first place.

In my case, I began with a sincere heart and honest intentions of serving the Lord through service to those around me. However, as often happens, my ministry, rather than my relationship with the Lord and fellowship with His Spirit, took first place in my life. It wasn't a conscious decision I made that allowed this to happen; in fact, it happened over a period of time without my noticing . . . at least until things hit bottom. I woke up one day and realized that the freshness of my relationship with Jesus was gone, and that I pretty well hated everything I was doing related to serving and ministering to others. It was a harsh realization that caused me to pull out of ministry almost completely for several years. Gratefully, God continued to woo my heart throughout the process, bringing awareness of my diversion before it was too late.

Finally, it is important to realize that if we focus our heart on the first great commandment (loving God), then we will automatically conform to the second (loving others). We can't help it. You have likely heard someone make the statement, "So-and-so is too heavenly minded to be any earthly good." This is a declaration often made by well-intentioned individuals who have embraced God's heart for service and are concerned that someone spends too much time talking and praying about the problems around him without taking any action. It is based on a judgment that a certain person is so concerned about developing his relationship with Jesus that he has completely forgotten about the people and issues around him. Can I just say that in more than twenty years of ministry I have yet to find such a person? I believe there are two reasons why this is the case.

First, the overwhelming majority of us do not spend nearly the time and energy developing our relationship with God that we might allow others to believe. Most of us are not really all that "heavenly minded" at all. I believe this is beginning to change as God gives us more grace, but most of us still have a long way to go. Second, anyone who is truly heavenly minded and falling more in love with the Father cannot help but learn to love what He loves. The Scriptures are clear that God deeply loves His creation, so much so that He was willing to come in the form of a man and die for the redemption of our souls. How is it possible that we could not naturally grow in true love for other people as we grow in love for God? In my estimation, such a scenario is not possible.

Loving God Fully: Is "All" Really Possible?

Let's recall a verse from earlier. Jesus tells us in Mark 12:30 that we are to "love the Lord with all [our] heart, with all [our] soul, with all [our] mind, and with all [our] strength." The first thing I notice about Jesus' commandment is His liberal use of the word *all*. If I love him with *all* of my heart, mind, soul, and strength, then doesn't that mean none of those parts of me is left for anything else? Yep! He wants it all, and He is not willing to settle for anything less.

In Exodus 34:14 we are told that "the Lord, whose name is Jealous, is a jealous God." He desires so deeply to reveal Himself to us as more than just our savior, healer, and master, but the revelation of Jesus as our Bridegroom cannot be fully made known until He has all of us. He knows that full well, and that is why He is relentless in His pursuit of just this. As I said earlier, God wants us to love Him with all that we are precisely because He loves us with all that *He* is. Our love is both our debt and gift to God, and His requirement of our love is for our own benefit. It is only in giving Him all of our love that we experience that which we were truly created for and are able to love others in a way that goes beyond selfishness and blind emotion.

It is critical that you realize the only person in the world who can give Jesus all of *your* love is *you*! A unique part of Jesus' inheritance has been entrusted by the Father specifically to you. It is the love that only you can give. What's more, we get only a brief opportunity to voluntarily give this love to Him in a fallen world in which love for Jesus is both costly and rare. When we join with all the saints in worship before His throne in the age to come, everyone will be fully devoted in love to Jesus. While He will still fully cherish our love for Him, it will no longer be unique in the sense that it is an uncommon gift.

We have an opportunity to love Jesus now in a way that we never will again—to be lovesick for the One we cannot yet see.

However, to be lovesick for Jesus means that we seek to love Him in a deep and focused way rather than just "on the run" as we pursue other pleasures. It means that we desire an encounter with Him more than anything else, including success in ministry. It means we recognize our deep need for Him and are pained when we allow sin and compromise to get in the way (Matthew 5:3-4). It means that we cry out to Jesus to come to us as the jealous God who demands everything. As we cry, "Lord, we want more of You," He responds by saying, "And I want *all* of you!"

WE HAVE AN OPPORTUNITY TO LOVE JESUS NOW IN A WAY THAT WE NEVER WILL AGAIN—TO BE LOVESICK FOR THE ONE WE CANNOT YET SEE.

So, what does it mean for us to love God with all our heart, all our soul, all our mind, and all our strength? While I think the answer to that question is probably a little different for each of us, I will try to provide at least a general overview in the chapters that follow. I think it will be helpful to begin by looking at an example of someone who dared to love Jesus with everything that was in her. Maybe by looking at her example we will gain some insights that will allow us to be more devoted lovers ourselves.

Chapter Four

LOVING GOD WITH ALL OUR HEART: A CASE STUDY

"I don't want to just serve Him. I want to be obsessed
with this Man who's on the throne."

–Mike Bickle

How many times have we heard someone use the phrase, "I love you with all of my heart?" Maybe you have said these words to someone. What are we trying to communicate when we use such language? Although it is probably not true in the majority of cases, what we are saying to that person is we love him or her with everything that we have. We are pledging all that we are belongs to him or her, and that we have a deep longing to be with that person, a strong desire to know him or her more intimately, and an emotional connection to this person we love that we can't communicate with lesser words. Our minds are constantly set on that person, we conduct ourselves in a way that communicates our love, and we do not hesitate to give of our resources—whether time, money, or anything else—so that the object of our affections will know that we are truly in love with them! This is exactly the way Jesus tells us we are to love Him!

When we talk about loving God with all our heart, the word *heart* speaks of our emotions, affections, and longings— the very impulse of desire that affects every decision we make and every action we take. The heart is the hidden current that directs the course of our inner being. It is what makes human-kind unique, set apart from every other created being (even angels are not described in Scripture as having affections). It is at the center of who we are and defines our core reality. That is the reason the Scriptures command us to "Keep [our] heart with all diligence, for out of it spring the issues of life" (Proverbs 4:23).

Of the four spheres of life in which Jesus commands us to love Him (heart, soul, mind, strength), the heart is the most difficult to delineate because so much is wrapped up in that simple word. Although Jesus isolates the heart as one of four specific areas in which we are to love God, in some ways it could be seen as a type of summary of the other three: loving God with all of our heart requires loving Him with all of our soul, mind, and strength.

While we can't directly affect our hearts—we don't just sud-denly decide to have strong emotions and affections toward someone or something—we can set our hearts toward loving whatever we choose, and our emotions will eventually follow wherever we set ourselves to pursue. In other words, we can determine the course in which our emotions develop over time. It does not happen overnight, and for those who have experienced trauma or emotional abuse, the path may seem especially arduous. Be patient with yourself. Associate with people who will encourage you along the way. Don't be afraid or embarrassed to ask for any help you need. Rest in the fact that as we change our goals and our actions, the Holy Spirit is faithful to change our hearts. Yet we must play our part. Sitting idly by and wishing that we would become passionate lovers is naive and unfruitful. Sincerity is critical, but it is not enough.

Setting our hearts on God includes both cultivating that which enlarges our capacity to love and removing all that diminishes our affections. When God created Adam and Eve, he placed them in a garden called Eden, a paradise that served as the place in which God would commune with His creation in a very real and intimate way. It is interesting that God gave Adam and Eve a single task that was to occupy their time and attention: tend the garden. Just as the garden was the place of encounter for the first humans, our hearts are now the place where we commune with God through the inner working of His Spirit. And once again, God gives us one primary task with which we are to be concerned: tending the garden!

AND ONCE AGAIN, GOD GIVES US ONE PRIMARY TASK WITH WHICH WE ARE TO BE CONCERNED: TENDING THE GARDEN!

We fertilize and water the garden of our heart by spending time in the Word, developing a rich prayer life, fasting, and enjoying biblical fellowship with other believers, among other things. We weed our gardens by removing distractions such as bitterness, lust, over-stimulation by entertainment, and the pursuit of acquiring material possessions and influence. Often the weeds that would choke out our gardens do not come in the form of obvious sin; however, distractions that might not be considered "bad" can hijack our attention and affections. Paul addresses this reality in 2 Corinthians 11:3 when he writes, "I am afraid that just as Eve was deceived by the serpent's cunning, your minds may somehow be led astray from your sincere and pure devotion to Christ." I am convinced that Satan is not nearly as concerned with what we *do* with our lives as he is with what we *don't* do. He doesn't so much care whether you commit adultery or murder as he does that you don't love God with all of your heart. He loves it when the church concerns itself with doctrinal arguments, programming, or any other distraction from loving our Bridegroom.

Like King David, we must make a conscious decision to love God with all of our heart and then order our lives around that goal. David said in Psalm 18:1, "I *will* love you, O Lord, my strength." He made up his mind that he was going to be a lover of God and then set his heart to love Him by committing to walk in obedience, even when it was costly. He made every effort to set aside meaningless distractions, choosing instead to "delight himself in the Lord." Remember, it was David who penned the often-misinterpreted line, "Delight yourself also in the Lord, and He shall give you the desires of your heart" (Psalm 37:4). It seems to me that if we are truly delighted in something, then that thing *has become* the desire of our heart. It is as if God were saying through David, "If you will delight yourself in me, I will give you what you desire . . . more of me!"

If we set our hearts to love God by regularly asking for supernatural help to love Jesus, then He promises that the Holy Spirit will see to it that our love grows stronger over time. That is why Paul prayed for the Thessalonians that the Lord would "direct [their] hearts into the love of God" (2 Thessalonians 3:5). He also writes in Romans 5:5: "The love of God has been poured out in our hearts by the Holy Spirit." As I mentioned in an earlier chapter, it takes God to love God, so I would encourage you to ask the Holy Spirit to pour the Father's love for Jesus into your heart and to direct your heart into His love.

Pursuing Intimacy: Sitting at His Feet

To help us fully understand what it looks like to set our hearts on loving Jesus, I want to take a look at an individual from Scripture who made knowing and worshiping Jesus the primary pursuit of her life. If anyone understood what it means to "delight [herself] in the Lord," this person did. She is a person whose life I almost completely overlooked for quite some time, but in the past few years she has become one of the most inspiring personalities in the New Testament to me.

My heart is certainly stirred as I read the accounts of John the Baptist, the one about whom Jesus Himself said, "among those born of women there has not risen anyone greater" (Matthew 11:11). I cannot help but be moved by the writings of Paul the apostle, a man who traveled the ancient world telling people about Jesus and who experienced incredible suffering because of his devotion to the Lord. However, when we speak of what it looks like to be completely devoted to growing in love for Jesus, we cannot overlook a certain young girl from the Scriptures: Mary of Bethany.

Mary was a young woman whose life was marked by complete devotion to and love for Jesus. She is not mentioned a significant number of times in Scripture, but in each account of her life we learn a great deal about what it means to love the Lord with all our heart. The first account of Mary's life is found in Luke 10:38-42:

> As Jesus and his disciples were on their way, he came to a village where a woman named Martha opened her home to him. She had a sister called Mary, who sat at the Lord's feet listening to what he said. But Martha was distracted by all the preparations that had to be made. She came to him and asked, "Lord, don't you care that my sister has left me to do the work by myself? Tell her to help me!"
> "Martha, Martha," the Lord answered, "you are

worried and upset about many things, but only one thing is needed. Mary has chosen what is better, and it will not be taken away from her" (NIV).

It is important to realize that although Jesus does gently reprimand Martha, He is not correcting her for being a servant. Jesus Himself has the heart of a servant (Philippians 2), and He is seeking a church that will be a like-minded partner. However, it is absolutely critical that servanthood flow out of the experience of an intimate relationship with Jesus. Otherwise, the result is most often that we become bitter and burned out. While we may not realize it, it is possible for us to allow *serving* God (and others) to replace *knowing* and *experiencing* Him. That is the mistake Martha made. She does not do anything wrong by serving Jesus, but she did not realize the importance of choosing what Mary chose—to sit at His feet and get to know Him. Because she failed to connect with Jesus at the heart level, her serving became burdensome to her, and she lashed out in anger at both Mary and Jesus. Jesus lovingly corrected her, pointing out that what Mary had chosen was the "one thing that is needed" and that "it will not be taken away from her."

I believe Mary's choice and Jesus' correction of Martha serve as a strong warning to us, especially in a world that places a high value on movement and getting things done. We live in a society in which accomplishment equals worth—those who "accomplish" more are to be admired. Jesus counters by placing a higher value on sitting at His feet, listening to

> WHILE WE MAY NOT REALIZE IT, IT IS POSSIBLE FOR US TO ALLOW *SERVING* GOD (AND OTHERS) TO REPLACE *KNOWING* AND *EXPERIENCING* HIM. THAT IS THE MISTAKE MARTHA MADE.

what He says, and knowing Him intimately. This is just one of the many areas in which civilization and the kingdom of God clash, and we must be careful to choose wisely how we will spend our time. Although there are other good things, other important things we should not ignore, there is only one essential thing—knowing and worshiping Jesus!

When we choose to put aside the distractions of life, whether they be sinful or simply other "good things," determining instead to focus our attention on Jesus, He counts it as true worship. Although worship certainly may take the form of singing songs to the Lord when we gather together on a Sunday morning for "worship service," it is not the singing itself that forms the basis for worship. True worship is found in choosing God over all other options that flood our lives and by focusing all that we have and all that we are on knowing and loving Him. This is what Mary did, and Jesus called it a beautiful and necessary thing.

Extravagance: "Wasting" Our Lives on Jesus

A few years ago I read a book, *Don't Waste Your Life,* by one of my favorite authors and teachers, John Piper. The premise of the book is that we waste our lives when we live with the goal of making much of ourselves rather than making much of God. Piper writes, "God created us to live with a single passion to joyfully display his supreme excellence in all the spheres of life. The wasted life is the life without this passion."[5] God created us to worship Him and to live in intimate relationship with Him, and to the degree that we fall short of this, our lives are wasted. It is also important to note that God is interested in more than our simply meeting the "minimum

---

[5] John Piper, *Don't Waste Your Life* (Wheaton, IL: Crossway Books, 2003), 37.

requirements." He desires a people marked by their extravagance and extreme devotion.

I think Piper has it right when he says that we waste our lives when we do not make it our driving purpose to make much of Jesus; however, we might also say that we have not truly lived unless we *do* waste our lives—in extravagant devotion to Him. To illustrate, let's take a look at yet another event in the life of Mary of Bethany:

> Now the Passover and the Feast of Unleavened Bread were only two days away, and the chief priests and the teachers of the law were looking for some sly way to arrest Jesus and kill him. "But not during the Feast," they said, "or the people may riot."
> While he was in Bethany, reclining at the table in the home of a man known as Simon the Leper, a woman came with an alabaster jar of very expensive perfume, made of pure nard. She broke the jar and poured the perfume on his head (Mark 14:1-3, NIV).

Let's stop for a minute and examine what is taking place. To avoid any confusion, we know that the woman in this story is none other than the same Mary who sat at the feet of Jesus in Luke 10. We know this because she is identified as such in another telling of the same story in John 12. The event takes place two days before the Passover, which is only a couple of days before Jesus is arrested and crucified. Mary enters the house of Simon the Leper with a jar of perfume that we are told has a value equivalent to a year's wages for an average worker. (Bible scholars estimate the present-day value of the perfume to be in the neighborhood of $20,000.) This perfume likely represented everything of value that Mary had to her name. It was not normal for such a young woman to own something as valuable as the nard perfume, so it was likely an inheritance that Mary had received from her deceased parents (we are never introduced to them in any story concerning Mary and Martha). This assumption is further supported by the fact that the house that Mary lived in is described as "the house of Martha" in Luke 10. In Mary's day, women were never considered to be the owner of the home unless they were the only ones who lived there. Furthermore, unless it was given to them in an inheritance, women, especially ones as young as Mary and Martha, were unable to afford a house.

Depending on whether you read the account in Mark 14 or John 12, we are told that Mary poured the perfume either on Jesus' head or on His feet. My guess is that with as much perfume as Mary had, she poured it on His head and it ran down His body onto His feet. Whatever the case, she completely "wastes" the perfume through what she has done, at least in the eyes of the others in attendance. What's more, John 12:3 tells us that once Mary has poured out her offering on Jesus, she kneels at His feet and begins to wipe them with her hair. Even with little understanding of the culture during that time, we can see that Mary humbled herself in a way that was undignified and improper for the setting in which she found herself. However, when we read in 1 Corinthians 11:15 that a woman's long hair is "her glory," the story takes on an even deeper significance. In effect, what Mary is doing here is proclaiming through her actions that she considers everything she has and everything she is to be of value only as it is useful for loving and worshiping Jesus.

Whether it was because they were simply uncomfortable with the events that took place or because they were convicted by the extravagance of Mary's act of worship, those who saw what Mary had done were annoyed and offended.

Some of those present were saying indignantly to one another, "Why this waste of perfume? It could have been sold for more than a year's wages and the money given to the poor." And they rebuked her harshly.

"Leave her alone," said Jesus. "Why are you bothering her? She has done a beautiful thing to me. The poor you will always have with you, and you can help them anytime you want. But you will not always have me. She did what she could. She poured perfume on my body beforehand to prepare for my burial. I tell you the truth, wherever the gospel is preached throughout the world, what she has done will also be told, in memory of her" (Mark 14:4-9, NIV).

I love Jesus for a great number of reasons, and one of the most special is found in this passage. It touches my heart deeply to know that Jesus takes it personally when the people around Mary begin to scold her for her extravagance. Jesus is very quick to tell them, "Leave her alone! What you call waste, I count as love, and I don't appreciate your messing with my friend!" He is touched by the act of extravagant worship that Mary demonstrates, and He cannot remain silent when the insults begin to fly in her direction. Not only does he tell her critics to shut up, He also points out that Mary will be remembered for eternity because of what she has done! Imagine how much of a bubble buster that must have been for the arrogant observers. I can imagine Jesus saying, "Hey Bartholomew, you may be one of the Twelve, but people will have a hard time even remembering your name. Andrew, you've spent a great deal of time with me, but not much will be said of you. But Mary . . . oh, she has touched my heart in a special way, and she will be remembered for eternity." And apparently, Jesus was right since we are talking about her today.

Jesus desires for us to experience intimacy with Him, and He wants us to live in the freedom of wasting our lives on Him without regard for the cost. You may not be rich in a financial sense, but you possess the most costly asset a person can own: your heart. In fact, it is so costly Jesus gave His life to redeem it! You are the only one who can choose to give your heart to Him, and when you throw caution to the wind in doing so, He calls it "a beautiful thing." And when we relate to Jesus in extravagance, it opens the door to our experiencing Him in a way others cannot. Notice that after Mary finished anointing Jesus with the perfume, there were only

> SHE LOVED JESUS WITH SUCH A PASSION THAT EVERYTHING ELSE IN HER LIFE BECAME MEANINGLESS BY COMPARISON. SHE HAD JESUS, AND FOR HER THAT WAS ENOUGH.

two people in the room whose bodies were covered with the fragrance: Jesus and Mary. After she has lavished her love on Jesus, Mary is identified with Him in a way unlike anyone else in the room.

Friendship With God

What sets Mary apart from so many others is that she understood what it meant to be a friend to Jesus. She pursued intimacy with Him with all her being. Mary was not a Bible scholar, and she didn't understand the mysteries that Peter, James, and John were beginning to see, but she loved Jesus with such a passion that everything else in her life became meaningless by comparison. She had Jesus, and for her that was enough. Furthermore, she was apparently the only one who really listened and understood what Jesus had been saying time and time again about His death, burial, and resurrection. While others at the table stood and judged her, Mary anointed Jesus for burial, not only with her expensive perfume, but also with her tears and love. Jesus was left with only one word to describe what she had done: "beautiful."

It is worth noting that there are really only three accounts of Mary's life that are recorded in Scripture. We have looked at two of these in some detail. The first is found in Luke 10, in which Mary is sitting at Jesus' feet listening intently to what He is saying. The second is the story of her anointing Jesus with her precious perfume. The third account is found in John 11. It is the familiar story of Jesus raising Mary's brother Lazarus from the dead four days after his death. We will not examine this story here, and I only mention it to point out a significant trend related to Mary's encounters with Jesus.

> I BELIEVE JESUS WAS CRYING BECAUSE ONE OF HIS BEST FRIENDS WAS HURTING DEEPLY, AND IT BROKE HIS HEART.

Read the stories again, this time paying special attention to where Mary is in relation to Jesus each of the three times. In the Luke 10 account, Mary is sitting at Jesus' feet. In Mark 14 we find Mary wiping Jesus' feet with her hair. And in the account of Lazarus, when Jesus arrives on the scene after his friend Lazarus has been in the tomb for several days, while Martha begins conversing with Jesus about what has taken place, Mary simply walks up and falls at His feet. We are then told that as Jesus looks down and sees Mary weeping, He too begins to weep. While there are numerous religious reasons we might employ to explain why Jesus begins to cry, I'm not convinced any of them suffice. I think the reason Jesus begins to weep is simple. I believe Jesus was crying because one of His best friends was hurting deeply, and it broke His heart. Jesus expressed His steadfast love for Mary in a beautiful way by crying alongside her.

We know from the Bible that Jesus loves everyone, but Mary was able to enter into a deeper, intimate, friendship kind of love that is available to anyone, but only a few ever experience. I think that is why, when Jesus entered the town of Bethany just six days before He was to be crucified, He spent all six nights at Mary's house. Imagine the strategic hour in which

Jesus found Himself and what He could have accomplished by spending the final days before His death with someone like Nicodemus, one of the top religious leaders of the day. Because of the Passover celebration, there were so many "important" people in Jerusalem at the time surrounding Jesus' death that you might expect Him to spend His time with, but it's almost as if Jesus instead says, "No, I want to be at Mary's house. I've got six days, and a very painful and troubling time before me, and I want to be with Mary because she understands and loves me." This may not be exactly the way things went down, but it seems like a very strong possibility based on what we read of the relationship between Mary and Jesus. Which leads me to ask myself the difficult question: "Would Jesus have any interest at all in spending His last week before the crucifixion at my house?"

Mary was never a preacher, and she never had a prominent ministry, but Jesus wanted to be with her due to her single-minded devotion to Him. In fact, you might say that Mary "wasted" her life on Jesus. But when it comes down to it, we all end up wasting our lives somehow. We cannot hold on to our lives and save them. We can waste them in sin if we choose. We can waste them in mediocrity. Or we can dare to "waste" them on Jesus. The question each of us has to answer is not *if* we will waste our life, but *how* we will waste it. Growing in friendship with Jesus seems like a pretty appealing option to me.

Chapter Five

LOVING GOD WITH ALL OUR MIND

"What comes into our minds when we think about God is
the most important thing about us."

–A.W. Tozer, *The Knowledge of the Holy*[6]

After examining the life of Mary of Bethany, I can only assume
that each of us who has said a legitimate yes to the Holy Spirit's
leading in our lives would want to love God in much the same
way Mary did. However, we are immediately faced with a difficult question: How? How can we possibly steer our immature
hearts toward complete fascination and devotion? It has been
my experience that it is almost, if not completely, impossible
to affect our hearts directly in such a way that we are suddenly
overwhelmed with passionate love for Jesus. However, there
are certain spheres of wholehearted love that we can directly
influence. As we focus on making small but real changes in

[6] Tozer, *The Knowledge of the Holy*, 1.

each of these areas, our hearts are changed.

The primary avenue by which we are able to transform our affections is through the renewing of the mind. We can set our emotions on becoming wholehearted lovers of God, but then we must feed those emotions through giving our minds in loving devotion to the things of God. If we just wish that our hearts will be suddenly and radically abandoned to Jesus, then we will likely not experience much change. However, if we begin with an earnest desire to love God completely, and then engage in the process of becoming wholehearted lovers by feeding our mind on truth, as our mind is transformed, so our heart will be also.

One of the primary ways we love God with our mind is to meditate on His written Word. This is an absolutely essential component for growing in passion for Jesus. While this may seem obvious to most of us, it is astounding how few have actually set aside sufficient time to participate in devotional study on a regular basis. Moreover, most of us who have made spending time in the Word a priority in our daily lives have no focused plan of attack for engaging the Scriptures in a meaningful way. If focused and intentional time in meditation is to our maturing in love as fuel is to the car, then it is no wonder many of our hearts have never left the driveway.

It is important to remember that loving God with our mind includes meditating on the Word, not simply reading it. Meditation involves reflecting on what we have read and engaging the Spirit in meaningful dialogue related to the content. While knowledge of the Scriptures is important, it should never be our goal merely to become a Bible scholar with exceptional academic understanding of the Word. The kind of knowledge we are to desire is of an experiential nature—we long for encounters with the Spirit of God through our time in meditation. Therefore, it is critical that we make Paul's prayer for the Ephesians (1:16-17) an integral part of our own prayer lives: "[I] do not cease . . . making mention of you in my prayers: that the . . . Father of glory, may give to you the spirit of wisdom and revelation in the knowledge of Him."

The Apostle Paul's heart came alive with fascination as he meditated on Jesus, the Word made flesh. Did you know that we have a right and an inheritance to live with that same fascination on every step of the journey? Yet if we are to fully grasp the richness of the Word of God, it is essential that we engage with the Holy Spirit, the One who is able to give us clarity and fullness in our understanding. It is only as we gain supernatural understanding of the Word that we are able to come into full agreement with who God is and how He views us and leads us.

WHILE IT IS GOD'S DESIRE THAT EACH OF US WOULD KNOW AND UNDERSTAND HIS HEART AND WAYS, THE SPIRIT DOES NOT GRANT SUCH REVELATION HASTILY OR CARELESSLY.

While it is God's desire that each of us would know and understand His heart and ways, the Spirit does not grant such revelation hastily or carelessly. We will find true delight in God only as we seek revelation of Him as one who seeks after hidden treasure: "My son, if you receive my words, and treasure my commands within you, so that you incline your ear to wisdom, and apply your heart to understanding; yes, if you cry out for discernment, and lift up your voice for understanding, if you seek her as silver, *and search for her as for hidden treasures;* then you will understand the fear of the Lord, and find the knowledge of God" (Proverbs 2:1-5, *emphasis mine*).

If we had the knowledge that a valuable treasure was buried somewhere in our own backyard, most of us would lose sleep and do whatever necessary to find and recover it. If we are honest, however, most of us would be forced to admit that we do not seek after revelation of God's heart in this way. As we discussed in an earlier chapter, God wants us to experience intimacy with His heart, but it will cost us something to do so, including our precious time. We can't simply plug seeking revelation of God into our schedules "when we have time" and expect a fruitful return from our efforts. Instead, God desires for us to make our pursuit of the knowledge of Him of primary importance and then to plan our schedule around that goal. If we live with the intention of spending focused time with the Lord if we happen to find some, I can assure you from personal experience that we never will! In order for our minds to grow in love, we must be committed to diligence in our time in the Word, relegating many of our current priorities to a lesser status and enjoying those options when the time happens to come available.

A key word in learning to love God with our minds is *intentionality*. We will more than likely not stumble onto revelation of God, but we are promised that it will be given to us as we intentionally seek it out. The Apostle Paul was very deliberate in His meditation on the character and ways of Jesus, and his heart was alive with fascination as a result: "Oh, the depth of the riches both of the wisdom and knowledge of God! How unsearchable are His judgments and His ways past finding out!" (Romans 11:33). It doesn't take an exhaustive study of Paul's life to see that his heart and mind were set on one thing—to know God's heart as fully as He would allow.

Paul was overwhelmed by the immenseness of the Godhead, stating that God's thoughts and ways were "unsearchable" and "beyond finding out." What Paul is communicating here is not that we are unable to know God; if that were the case, what would be the point of searching Him out? He is saying that we cannot know God *exhaustively*, as He is too big to wrap our finite minds around. That is why Paul had such depth of knowledge yet remained perpetually fascinated with God's character, emotions, thoughts, and ways. God has and will continue to make Himself known, but only to those who are committed to seeking Him with intentionality.

Tearing Down the "Love Blocks"

Part of being intentional in loving God with our minds includes removing the harmful attitudes and mindsets that diminish our love. While there is a large number of these "love blockers" that keep us from engaging in fully loving God with our minds—bitterness, lust, greed, anger, and many more—there are two that I believe to be the most prevalent and dangerous: shame and ingratitude.

I can't think of anything that paralyzes us, both in our growth in love and effectiveness in ministry, more than shame. Many of us believe the lie that if we really loved God, we wouldn't continue to give in to temptation and struggle with the sin patterns that we do. When we fall short, we are tempted to impose upon ourselves a period of suffering and probation before we feel "worthy" to get back in the game. Here's the truth: that type of thinking is deeply rooted in pride, not humility. The only one caught off guard by your sin is you, and no matter how long you resign yourself to the prison of shame and self-hatred, you will never be worthy to receive God's love or pursue anything in His name. You weren't worthy before your latest screwup, remember? But the

THE ONLY ONE CAUGHT OFF GUARD BY YOUR SIN IS YOU, AND NO MATTER HOW LONG YOU RESIGN YOURSELF TO THE PRISON OF SHAME AND SELF-HATRED, YOU WILL NEVER BE WORTHY TO RECEIVE GOD'S LOVE OR PURSUE ANYTHING IN HIS NAME.

good news is that "while we were still sinners, Christ died for us" (Romans 5:8).

Shame is a waste of time that minimizes love. God's original plan for man did not include shame, and our spirits cannot come alive when we choose to embrace it. Instead, our energies should be spent embracing the grace of repentance. Break your agreement with compromise and hold tight to your confession of Jesus' completed work on the cross! Confess your sin. Call it what it is and own it. Then receive your forgiveness, push the delete button, and get back in the game as a first-class citizen in God's kingdom. We cannot afford to "pay God back" for yesterday's sin. Why waste time trying when God gives us such a clear pathway toward a pure heart and clean conscience?

Equally as destructive, and much more difficult to detect, is the "love blocker" known as ingratitude. What is it within the consciousness of man that believes we deserve *anything* from the Lord? Most of us would say we don't believe that, yet our lives reflect that we do. Sure, if we have any amount of spiritual sensitivity at all, then we recognize God's hand in the "big" blessings. But what about the smaller ones? You know, like the very fact that we woke up this morning sucking oxygen. We are not owed even that, yet God is so gracious to continue to provide, even when we do not recognize His provision.

In Song of Solomon 2:6, the Shulamite says of the King that "His left hand is under my head, and his right hand embraces me." While this may sound like another one of the "PG-13" verses in the Song, its deeper meaning is critical. The right hand of the King (Jesus) is embracing her in a way she can easily discern. This speaks of the blessings of God that are obvious to us—or at least should be. In addition, the Shulamite also recognizes the left hand of the King. It is "under her head," meaning that it is providing support that she knows is there, even though she can't see it. This speaks of the provision of God that we are not aware of unless we deliberately choose to be.

Have you ever taken time to really sit down and consider where you would be if the devil had his way with you? If you choose to give even the slightest portion of your attention and affections to Jesus, the devil hates you, remember? Do you really think you have made it this far without some behind-the-scenes intervention from your Heavenly Father? Think about it. Meditate on it. Are you feeling gratitude welling up in your heart even now? Just think how differently we would live if we continually discerned and meditated on *both* arms of our Bridegroom. Ingratitude flourishes in a mind that is disengaged from loving God, but it cannot survive in the mind that is intentionally fixed on His goodness.

The Power of the Renewed Mind

We know from Genesis 1:26 that when God created man, He created us in His own image and likeness. While that image and likeness has been heavily marred by the entrance of sin into the equation, the foundational elements of creation are still in place. One aspect of this reality can be easily seen in the vastness of the internal universe known as the human mind. The mind is more powerful than most of us realize. In fact, science reveals that even the most brilliant geniuses only use a very small fraction of the power their minds possess. It is no wonder that Jesus tells us we are to learn to love God with all our minds! And it is no wonder that the enemy will stop at nothing to capture our attention. Where our attention goes, our minds follow. Powerful potential for both good and evil rests in the mind, and we must be careful to guard it diligently.

We can think of the mind as being a 24/7 movie studio in which we are the primary producer, actor, and audience. Because of our ability to both remember and imagine, our minds constantly rotate through vast reservoirs of images that we have either stored or created. Even when we are not the direct subject of these thought pictures, they are still typically tied to our relationships and interactions with the subject. As we watch the movie begin to unfold, we are constantly making decisions about which images to give our attention. It is through this dual role of actor and audience that we ultimately become the producer, generating even more internal images that are in the same vein as those we deem worthy of our gaze. Surely you can see how this mental cinema can be either a blessing or a curse, depending on the subject matter in the films we are cranking out.

EVEN WHILE WE SLEEP, THE FILM STILL ROLLS. THIS IS NOT BY ACCIDENT. GOD CREATED US WITH THIS CAPACITY TO ALLOW FOR CEASELESS DIALOGUE WITH HIM.

We are constantly engaged in a never-ending conversation in our minds. In fact, a significant portion of our lives is spent within our minds simply because we can never shut them off. Even while we sleep, the film still rolls. This is not by accident. God created us with this capacity to allow for ceaseless dialogue with Him. Through the miracle of memory and imagination, we are able interact with the Lord without interruption, even if much of the interaction is at a subconscious level. Therein lies the beauty and power of the renewed mind.

In Romans 12:2, Paul tells us that we are to constantly be transformed by the "renewing of our minds." Since our minds define so much of who we are and how we love, this renewing process is essential. Without it, our tendency is to continue to produce films that cause us to "walk in futility" and have our "understanding darkened" (Ephesians 4:17-23). However, through the redemptive work of Jesus and the presence of the

Holy Spirit in the life of the believer, we have the capacity to supernaturally erase the horror films marked by the hurt of what has happened *to* us and the shame of what has happened *through* us and replace them with new films that bring life and peace. What an incredible opportunity! Yet, so many of us choose not to accept it, either because we don't believe it is possible or because we are unwilling to invest the time and energy necessary to realize the transformation.

Loving God with our whole mind *is* a supernatural possibility! Through mediation on the Word and the goodness of God in our lives, we can take the reins of our minds and write the script of the movie that we continually watch within. We cannot shut down the images that constantly scroll through our minds, but we absolutely can redirect them. However, this certainly doesn't happen overnight. There is a process and a pace which the Lord determines. However, we can trust that His leadership is good and that He will give grace to our commitments that are made according to His will. It is His great desire that Jesus becomes our first thought, our holy daydream, and our sweet escape from lust, pride, bitterness, fear, anger, and any other thought or emotion that hinders love. He wants to be our resting place, the One to whom our thoughts naturally turn as we go through our day.

Of course, all of this only happens to the degree that we truly desire it. We cannot expect lasting change by pursuing holiness even a majority of the time if we are actively engaged in compromise at other times. As I mentioned in an earlier chapter, I am not referring to slipups that are the result of immaturity, but to the spirit of rebellion that seeks to convince us that we can purposely push God aside for a time in order to pursue our own carnal appetites. This rebellious spirit is fueled by the "cheap grace" message that has become so prevalent, especially in the Western Church.

Dietrich Bonhoeffer, a German pastor, theologian, author,

and martyr, wrote the modern classic, *The Cost of Discipleship*. In it, he wrote: "Cheap grace is the preaching of forgiveness without requiring repentance, baptism without church discipline, Communion without confession, absolution without personal confession. Cheap grace is grace without discipleship, grace without the cross, grace without Jesus Christ, living and incarnate."[7] We must be diligent to guard our hearts against this demonic doctrine and any other idea that "exalts itself against the knowledge of God, bringing every thought into captivity to the obedience of Christ" (2 Corinthians 10:5). So much life and time is wasted in our mind. It is tragic how many hours the average person wastes away in dreaming of that which is not based on truth. But we were not created to be average!

Forgetting and Remembering

Loving God with our minds entails a constant process of choosing to forget or remember, and the catalyst for this process is a continual and deliberate feeding of our minds on truth. For most of us, the majority of our thoughts are related to our pasts. God has graced us with an uncanny ability to remember, and that memory is intended to be a blessing. The Scriptures consistently remind us to remember the encounters God has initiated with His people, both personally and with others throughout history. As we reflect on His goodness, we are empowered to face the future with boldness and strength.

At the same time, there are certain things that the Scriptures command us to forget. The Apostle Paul says in Philippians 3:13-14, "One thing I do, *forgetting* those things which are

---

[7] Dietrich Bonhoeffer, *The Cost of Discipleship* (New York, NY: Touchstone, 1995), 44, 45.

behind and reaching forward to those things which are ahead, I press toward the goal for the prize of the upward call of God in Christ Jesus." What types of things did Paul find it necessary to forget? First, I believe Paul understood the importance of learning from our past failures and then cutting them loose. Although we may not be able to completely wipe them from our memory, we can choose not to focus on and identify ourselves by our mistakes and shortcomings. In addition, given the context of the passage in which Paul's words are found, I believe Paul also found it necessary to let go of and forget the things he once considered to be of more value than knowing Jesus—the things he gave up in order to follow the call of God on his life.

Unfortunately, our natural tendency is to remember the things we are supposed to forget and forget the things we are supposed to remember! This is a significant problem given that our ability to love God is related to how we view our past, either negatively or positively. Clinging to negative experiences and failing to seek out the good that God has brought out of our pain results in a bitterness that leads us to wrong paradigms about both God and ourselves. It locks our hearts from receiving love from God and returning it back to Him. However, when we choose instead to discern the truth about God's goodness in our past, the ways He has forgiven, delivered, and provided for us, we develop hearts of gratitude, and this is the only foundation upon which legitimate love for God is built.

So, if it is true that a healthy process of forgetting and remembering is essential in growing in love and passion for Jesus, doesn't it make sense that the devil would attempt to keep us locked in the cage of bitterness and ingratitude? Satan's plan is to cause the negative events of our past to remain alive in our memory as a destructive force while causing the positive realities of God's goodness to be forgotten. What's worse is that our natural mind tends toward agreeing with the enemy's deception. Negative events from our past, whether we were the victim or perpetrator, are never simply forgotten. There is a necessary process of confession, forgiveness, and healing that must take place.

In the case of sin, we must acknowledge and declare war on it through repentance. The only ground that the enemy has for his accusations is unconfessed sin. We overcome those accusations by agreeing with God (repenting) and holding fast to truth, overcoming the devil "by the blood of the Lamb and by the word of [our] testimony" (Revelation 12:11). In the case of our being mistreated or enduring disappointments, we must learn to interpret our experiences according to the truth of God's Word through revelation granted by the Holy Spirit. If we allow ourselves to become offended as a result of our disappointments, we quickly become paralyzed in our growth in love. We instead begin to blame and accuse both God and other people, and it is impossible to love those whom you hold responsible for difficulties you have faced. That is why it is so critical that we gain a firm grasp on the realities of the bridal paradigm I discussed in Chapter 1.

Without an understanding of God's passion for us, His overall disposition toward us, and His unwavering desire to present His Son with a bride "without spot or wrinkle" (Ephesians 5:27), we cannot rightly interpret *any* of the events in our lives, especially the difficult ones. His leadership is perfect, and He can be trusted. Moreover, not only can we trust that He is for us, but we can also entrust our enemies to Jesus' great wisdom and power. When we choose the path of leaving vengeance to the Lord instead of striking back or holding a grudge, we identify with the One who, "when He was reviled, did not revile in return; when He suffered, He did not threaten, but committed Himself to Him who judges righteously" (1 Peter 2:23). That seems like a pretty good way to live!

Reaching Forward

IF OUR ONLY VISION FOR THE FUTURE IS BRINGING HOME A PAYCHECK, RAISING CHILDREN WHO WILL ONE DAY BE GOOD CITIZENS, AND SITTING IN A WORSHIP SERVICE FOR AN HOUR OR TWO EACH WEEK, THEN WE ARE DOOMED, AS THOREAU MUSED, TO "LEAD LIVES OF QUIET DESPERATION."

In addition to forgetting those things which were behind him, Paul said he was also "reaching forward" to those things that were ahead. His focus was on the future, and since he was well acquainted with the character of God and trusted that His leadership is perfect, Paul's heart was filled with an inextinguishable hope. It was this hope, combined with a lovesick heart, which empowered Paul to remain steady through overwhelming circumstances and persecution. While his earthly circumstances were almost never desirable, Paul understood that his citizenship truly was in Heaven, and he looked forward to being reunited with Jesus in his resurrected body.

Our present—the way we think and feel today—is anchored in how we picture our future. Yet most people are ambivalent at best when it comes to what lies ahead. No wonder much of the church is marked by passionless ritual. If our only vision for the future is bringing home a paycheck, raising children who will one day be good citizens, and sitting in a worship service for an hour or two each week, then we are doomed, as Thoreau mused, to "lead lives of quiet desperation."[8] This hardly describes the lovesick bride of whom Jesus is worthy

---

[8] Henry David Thoreau, *Walden, Volume 1* (Boston: Houghton, Mifflin and Company, 1854), 15.

and deserving!

Creating a vision for our future that is firmly grounded in the Word of God is a dynamic part of loving God with our mind, because such a vision will naturally stir our spirits to go wholeheartedly after Jesus without hesitation or apology. We love Jesus today to the degree that we are able to think rightly about our future. What we believe about our future and the commitments we make based on those beliefs *dramatically* influence our capacity to love God. I am not necessarily talking about what we believe about our circumstances or the commitments we make to bettering our positions or environment, although I am all for positive thinking and striving for excellence in everything to which we put our hand. Instead, the beliefs and commitments I am referring to are in regard to what we will one day be at a heart level with God. We have very little control when it comes to planning the future for our "outer man," but with the aid of the Holy Spirit, we can plan the future for our "inner man" with 100 percent confidence.

If we do not have a clear picture for who we want to become over time, we will live carelessly with that time. "Where there is no revelation, the people cast off restraint" (Proverbs 29:18). In other words, those who do not have a life vision based on the Word of God will cast off discipline. The King James Version states the same truth in even more dramatic fashion: "Where there is no vision, the people perish" (Proverbs 29:18). Commitment to a life vision is critical, especially for followers of Jesus, because our commitments define so much of who we are. Sadly, many in the body of Christ are living in the midst of complete identity crises because they have no clearly defined commitment for the future.

It is almost impossible to maintain discipline and direction if you have no clear picture of who you are to become. Several times through the years I have made a commitment to a disciplined diet and exercise schedule. The times I have kept that commitment for more than a week were those times I was able to keep my focus on the level of health I was attaining rather than on the chicken fried steak I was not. And each time I have gradually slipped away from health-conscious routines, it has been because I lost focus of who I was becoming. That same reality is true in relation to our growth in love and passion for Jesus. We embrace the necessary disciplines such as prayer, fasting, and studying the Word much easier with clear visions of what our future can be in God. What we believe about where we are going and who we are becoming has significant bearing on how we live and relate to God today.

To be clear, I'm not talking about discipline for the sake of discipline. Ultimately, it is really all about hope! The reason we perish with no vision is because that lack of vision results in a lack of hope, and without hope the human psyche cannot flourish in anything, let alone passion for Jesus. On the other hand, if our hope *in* God is strong, our hearts cannot help but expand in love *for* God.

The work of Dr. Viktor Frankl, an Austrian neurologist and psychiatrist who survived the horrors of the Nazi concentration camps, provides us with great insight into the human mind and heart in relation to our ability to hope. Frankl rejected the hypothesis of his predecessor, Dr. Sigmund Freud, who he believed overemphasized the past as being the primary force that forms who we become. After the war, Frankl analyzed survivors of the Holocaust and categorized them into two broad categories: those who were emotionally stable and those who were not. He found that the predominant factor in the level of mental stability for those who came out of the concentration camps was not the horrors of what they experienced, but rather what they believed about their future. Those who maintained a healthy outlook in the midst of their torment and were able to remain hopeful about what was ahead were able to reassimilate and maintain and develop healthy relationships moving forward.[9]

People who embrace discipline because they have a clear vision and hope for the future live differently because they have different values. They spend their time differently. They spend their money differently. They are typically more easily able to shake off the passivity and lethargy that hold others back.

So, what are your goals for spiritual development? By all means, please set goals for your family, career, ministry, and other areas of life as well, but do not neglect that which is of the utmost importance! What are you determined to be in God? Paul prayed time and time again that the saints to whom he was writing (and those who would follow—that's us!) would be filled with the knowledge of God's will for them because he understood the power of a vision and strong commitment to the future. What do you believe God wants for you? How do you plan to get there?

WHAT DO YOU BELIEVE GOD WANTS FOR YOU? HOW DO YOU PLAN TO GET THERE?

Yes, it is ultimately the responsibility of the Holy Spirit to bring about sanctification and passion for Jesus, but we cannot fall into the presumptuousness that He will do it without our cooperation. The best news is, when we make intentional steps toward becoming everything that we can be in God because of how we think about both our past and our future, God counts that as love!

---

9 Viktor E. Frankl, *Man's Search for Meaning: An Introduction to Logotherapy* (New York: Simon and Schuster, 1984).

Chapter Six

LOVING GOD WITH ALL OUR SOUL

"Humility is the mother of giants. One sees great things
from the valley; only small things from the peak."

–G.K. Chesterton, *The Innocence of Father Brown*[10]

OK, now we turn to what I think may be the most challenging chapter in this book. It has literally taken me several months to finally sit down to write this one, and if I am honest, it is at least partly because I didn't want to be responsible for what I was learning. The deeper I have gone into this topic, the more I have realized how little my life aligns with the biblical definition of love—and that is the only definition that matters! As I have waded through the depths of what it means to love God with all of my soul and wrestled with the reality of my inability to do so, I have once again come face to face with His indelible grace and His promise that I *shall* love the Lord with all of my

---

[10] G.K. Chesterton, *The Innocence of Father Brown* (New York: John Lane Company, 1911), 255.

soul. It is from this place of confident brokenness that I hope to communicate something of worth to those who earnestly desire to love God with all that they are.

If we are to truly learn to love God with all of our heart, then we must cooperate with the Holy Spirit's process by which He teaches us to love God with all of our soul. Our soul is who we are at our core, and it is most clearly expressed through our personality. When I refer to *personality* here, I am not talking about traits such as loud or quiet, lighthearted or serious, and introverted or extroverted. I don't believe any of these traits is more holy than another, and I am convinced that God can use any combination of these types of traits for His glory. It *is* possible to love God wholeheartedly and be loud, quiet, lighthearted, serious, introverted, extroverted . . . but it is *not* possible to grow in love for God and be proud and unrestrained. Or maybe I should say it this way: we cannot simultaneously maintain a tenacious grasp on pride and self-centeredness while also growing in love. The two are mutually exclusive.

We express love for God (and others) by walking in humility in our attitudes and our speech. I confess, this is difficult for me. As I wrote at the beginning of this book, I am guilty of having spewed less-than-constructive criticism of pretty much everything under the sun, including the bride whom Jesus loves so dearly, His church. I am engaged in a perpetual wrestling match with my desire to be heard by others, and not only to be heard, but to be recognized as one who is worthy of their undivided attention and to whom they should submit their own ideas and will. But when we use phrases like "worthy of our devoted attention" and "submitting our will" in the context of our relationship with God, we might also find words like "worship" floating about in the conversation. Given that God will share His glory with no man, you can see how this poses an obvious problem for folks like me. You can also probably see why humility is essential, both as a catalyst for and a measure of our growth in love for God. And finally, you can probably see why I struggled to make myself actually write this chapter.

While our flesh fights vehemently against it, embracing humility is one theater the Father has chosen for us in which to express our love for Him. Each of us has a different struggle based on our personality and circumstances, and each of us has a slightly different assignment in how we express love for God in this way. Whatever our struggles, our costly choices to embrace meekness and humility touch the Father's heart in a way that few other actions can, primarily because we are choosing to identify with His nature and ways. The greatest form of affirmation is imitation, and our choices to crucify our flesh and embrace meekness are actually forms of worship. These choices are expressions of the value we place on God's heart, character, and leadership. They make it clear that we are willing to give up our "right" to *get ours* in order to *become His*, making a statement to the Lord that we will value humility simply because He values it.

No being will ever surpass God's power, and at the same time, no being will ever surpass His humility. The Father's humility is expressed in all that He does, and it is in His humility that His love is best displayed. "The Lord is high above all nations, His glory above the heavens. Who is like the Lord our God, Who dwells on high, Who humbles Himself to behold the things that are in the heavens and in the earth? He raises the poor out of the dust, and lifts the needy out of the ash heap, that He may seat him with princes—with the princes of His people" (Psalm 113:4-8). The One who created everything, rules over it all, and holds it all together is intimately aware of and concerned with the poor and needy. Our Father is humble, and because none is more powerful than He, none is more humble.

We see the same humility in the third Person of the Godhead, The Holy Spirit. While He is fully God, He chooses to work "behind the scenes" without desire to be recognized. He is happy in His humility. Look at Jesus' description of the Holy Spirit in John 16:13-14: "He will not speak on His own authority, but whatever He hears He will speak . . . He will glorify Me, for He will take of what is Mine and declare it to you." While He Himself is worthy of worship, the Holy Spirit's primary desire is to bring glory to the Father and the Son.

Speaking of the Son, there is probably no better, more obvious example of the humility of the Godhead than the life, ministry, death, and resurrection of Jesus. "No one has ever seen God, but the one and only Son, who is himself God and is in closest relationship with the Father, has made him known" (John 1:18, NIV). In Jesus we see perfectly the heart of the One who loves us fully and completely.

"Learn from Me . . . "

As with the other three spheres in which Jesus promises we will become wholehearted lovers of God (heart, mind, and strength), the reason God created us to love Him with all of our soul is because this is the way in which He loves us. At His core, God is a servant. You can't possibly understand the motives of Jesus and observe His ministry without being moved by His humility. He exerts no effort to be humble; it is not something He does, but who He is. During His ministry on earth, Jesus did not "put on" servanthood as a task or in order to make an example. He is a servant from eternity past. He did not serve because He had laid aside His power; He laid aside His power because he wanted to serve. It is precisely because Jesus was in the form of God that He sought to give and serve. He did not see washing the feet of those into whom He breathed life to be beneath Him, but viewed such lowly tasks as an opportunity to reveal who He really is: the humble Servant-God.

In Matthew 4:1-11, we read of an attempt by Satan to derail Jesus from His mission of redemption, and in this encounter, we are given a glimpse into the reality of Jesus' core identity of love expressed in humility. In this passage, Jesus is led by the Holy Spirit into the wilderness, where He engages in a forty-day fast. As the fast is drawing to an end, Satan approaches Jesus and attempts to convince Him to turn stones into bread. While I am sure Jesus must have been hungry after forty days without a bite, He counters Satan with the Word, answering, "It is written, 'Man shall not live by bread alone, but by every word that proceeds from the mouth of God'" (Matthew 4:4). Since Jesus deflects Satan by using Scripture, the tempter then challenges Jesus to throw Himself down from the highest point of the temple, using Scripture himself to "inform" Jesus that angels will protect Him if He is indeed the Son of God. Jesus, having a firmer grasp of the truth of God's Word (go figure!), once again shuts Satan down with truth, stating, "It is also written: 'Do not put the Lord your God to the test'" (Matthew 4:7, NIV). Finally, sensing that things are not going so well, Satan brings out the big guns. Knowing that Jesus is a king, Satan attacks Jesus with what he believes no king could turn down—the allure of riches and power. This is what appeals most to Satan, so he reasons that it must appeal to Jesus as well. Nope. Luckily for us, Jesus does not find His identity in power (although His is matchless), but in servanthood and humility. Therefore, He was not distracted by the appeal of

Satan, and we still have hope!

The life of the Godhead flows forever from a place of meekness, and Jesus put the riches of God's humility on clear display for all to see. Because He did so as a man under the anointing of the same Holy Spirit that dwells within the heart of every believer, understanding Jesus' humility both inspires and instructs us to seek the Spirit's power to help us love God in the same way in which He loves us. This is precisely why Jesus says, "Learn from Me, for I am gentle and lowly in heart" (Matthew 11:29). This is the only direct description Jesus gives of His own character, and He does so as a compassionate High Priest, knowing that we will struggle in this area and that walking out meekness will require the power found only in His example. How can One so strong stoop so low in such concern for His beloved? It is in considering this reality that we find strength to love in return!

THE LIFE OF THE GODHEAD FLOWS FOREVER FROM A PLACE OF MEEKNESS, AND JESUS PUT THE RICHES OF GOD'S HUMILITY ON CLEAR DISPLAY FOR ALL TO SEE.

Nowhere in Scripture are we given a better description of the humility and meekness of Jesus than in Paul's letter to the Church in Philippi:

> Let nothing be done through selfish ambition or conceit, but in lowliness of mind let each esteem others better than himself. Let each of you look out not only for his own interests, but also for the interests of others.
>
> Let this mind be in you which was also in Christ Jesus, who, being in the very form of God, did not consider it robbery ["something to be grasped," NIV] to be equal with God, but made Himself of no reputation, taking the form of a bondservant, and coming in the likeness of men. And being found in appearance as a man, He

humbled Himself and became obedient to the point of death, even the death of the cross (Philippians 2:3-8).

So, as we begin to look into what it means to love God with all of our soul, what we really must do is launch into a study of the character of Jesus. He was and is completely consumed with the interests of His Father, which should be our goal as well. In addition, because Jesus perfectly represents to us the heart of the Father, His humility and meekness awaken revelation as to how God really feels about us. That is our motivation. Consequently, in Jesus we find both the objective of and the inspiration for love.

"Reigning" It In

In examining the character and personality of Jesus, you may notice that the word "meekness" surfaces continually. Therefore, it is probably a good idea to establish a working definition of this term. In short, meekness is power and privilege under control. It speaks of restraint in the use of power, except in cases where that power is used to promote love. Now you can see why we can't possibly escape that term while considering who Jesus is at His core! However, it is important that we not make the mistake of confusing meekness with weakness, which is the absence of strength.

An analogy might be helpful to make this distinction. When you consider what it means to be meek, picture a horse under the restraint of a bridle. Pound for pound, there are few animals on earth more powerful than the horse, yet it is possible for even a child to climb onto a domesticated horse's back and lead the animal according to the much weaker rider's will. Does placing the bridle around the horse's neck somehow zap him of his great strength? Absolutely not! Yet as a result of time and training, the horse learns to submit his will to that of the rider, allowing himself to be led about by little more than a few feet of leather and a small piece of metal in his mouth. The great power of the beast is placed under the control of another. Meekness.

While this is a helpful analogy, I must confess that it falls significantly short in a number of ways when considering the meekness of Jesus. The horse is not naturally meek, but must be trained to submit to the rider's will. Jesus, on the other hand, considered it great joy to submit to His Father's will and serve not only the Father but us as well. As I said before, He does not have to work at being meek—it is who He is. This is precisely why He was able not only to humble Himself by becoming a man, but to take humility to an extreme by being beaten, ridiculed, and nailed to a tree in order to reconcile His beloved to Himself!

Since before time began, Jesus has existed in the form of God, distinguished from, yet equal to, the Father, eternally possessing all the glory and privilege of being God. The Apostle Paul tells us that Jesus is the very "image of the invisible God" (Colossians 1:15), and the author of Hebrews calls Jesus "the brightness of [the Father's] glory and the express image of His person" (Hebrews 1:3). Jesus Himself prayed to the Father in the Garden of Gethsemane: "Glorify Me together with Yourself, with the glory I had with You before the world was" (John 17:5). Jesus was, is, and always will be God; this must be understood. He shared in the Father's glory from the beginning, and in becoming a man and walking among us, Jesus did not, for one second, lose His deity. Instead, He laid aside the glory and privilege He enjoyed in Heaven, choosing only to exhibit power when the Holy Spirit came upon Him.

Jesus was God, yet He was hidden in the obscurity of humanity. He was our Creator, yet we didn't know him. As God, He chose not to draw on His own omnipotence, omnipresence, and omniscience. As a man, He lived completely dependent on the anointing of the Holy Spirit and prayer. Jesus possessed all the majesty of deity, performed all its functions, and enjoyed all of its prerogatives, yet He willingly made Himself vulnerable to pain, frustration, and humiliation. Why would God choose to lay aside glory and take the form of man, with complete knowledge of the extent to which He would suffer? Well, the obvious answer is His unfathomable love and inherent meekness. But that's not it . . . there's more!

While Jesus did not empty Himself of His deity when He became a man, He could not use His divine power for His own ends while on the earth and still qualify as our High Priest. In the Incarnation, Jesus now has two natures, being both fully God and fully man, with no contradiction. Jesus was never less than God, but He chose to restrain Himself and live as though He were never more than a man while He walked on the earth—a man anointed by the Holy Spirit through prayer. He willingly embraced a life of weakness, rejection, homelessness, poverty, weariness, shame, and pain. If He had stepped out of this, if He had faltered even for a moment, He would have been disqualified from being a human High Priest who was able to make a way for us. Our eternal destiny would have been eternally affected!

The author of Hebrews says it this way: "[I]n *all things* He had to be made like His brethren, that He might be a merciful and faithful High Priest in things pertaining to God, to make propitiation for the sins of the people" (Hebrews 2:17, *emphasis mine*). Jesus died as a perfect man so mankind might die to the power of sin without the justice of God being violated. He rose again as a man so we might walk in new life with Him. He defeated death and Hell as a man to take back the authority that was abdicated by the first man, Adam. And, as a man, He redefined what it means to live as a "mere man."

While fully God, Jesus did not consider the privileges associated with being equal to God as something to which

He should cling (Philippians 2:6). Thank God! Literally. No, seriously. Thank Him! While we see it is a scandal of injustice when we don't receive the honor we "deserve," Jesus refused to enjoy His unique privileges as God because He cared much more about pleasing His Father and redeeming His bride through obedient love. If this were not the case, we would be without hope. Jesus saw the incarnation as an opportunity to share with us the wealth of who He really is. His primary identity is that of a servant who is filled with love, so in denying Himself privileges and honor, He did not deny His core identity, but expressed His true heart of servanthood.

IS IT POSSIBLE THAT GOD'S POWER (AND WORTHINESS) *IS* BEST DISPLAYED WHEN A NATURALLY SELFISH MAN OR WOMAN SUBMITS HIS OR HER WILL TO HIS WAY OF HUMILITY?

When we see great works of power done in the name of Jesus, we are tempted to call it "the kingdom coming to earth." While I guess that is true, and while Jesus certainly manifested the power of God through the anointing of the Holy Spirit, the ministry of Jesus was and is primarily about love, humility, and the interests of others, and not just about power demonstrations. Is it possible that the "the kingdom coming to earth" really has more to do with followers of Jesus walking in humility and meekness than it does with displaying God's power? Or, better yet, is it possible that God's power (and worthiness) *is* best displayed when a naturally selfish man or woman submits his or her will to His way of humility? Jesus said we would do greater works than He did, so by all means, let's get to it! Yet as we do, let's not forget that our primary mandate is to love God and reflect His glory on earth. If Jesus chose to express love primarily through embracing humility and abandonment, then perhaps loving Him in return is deeply rooted in meekness as well.

Watch Your Mouth!

As a man anointed by the Holy Spirit, Jesus has given us the perfect example of a life lived with meekness and humility. As men and women anointed by the same Holy Spirit, we have the ability to walk as He walked, but not in our own power, of course. Most of us have tried that and come up short. I have. Over and over and over and . . . well, you get the point. We can't be zealous/passionate/ruined—or insert your favorite Christian buzzword here—enough even to approach the meekness of Jesus in our own strength. In fact, our zeal will, in time, typically lead us *away* from meekness. Instead, the power to live as Jesus lived is found in first dying with Him. Our flesh is neither humble nor meek. It will keep us from loving God with all of our soul. So, it must die. After its demise, we are free to live and love according to God's definition.

So how can we know if we are growing in our capacity to love God with all of our soul? The answer is actually quite simple. When you speak, listen. The extent to which we have allowed the Holy Spirit to kill our flesh and bring forth meekness in our hearts is best tested and proven in the area of our speech. Humility is an attitude of the heart, and there is perhaps no better window into our hearts than the words that pass over our lips. This is why Paul's application of his exhortation to the Philippians to *walk* in humility focuses on the need to *speak* with humility: "Therefore . . . work out your own salvation with fear and trembling. . . . Do all things without complaining and disputing, that you may become blameless . . . children of God without fault . . . holding fast the word of life" (Philippians 2:12-16).

Let's take a moment to pick this verse apart and see what

Paul is really telling us. First, he begins his statement with the word "therefore." If you will excuse the corny preacher humor for a moment, when we see the word "therefore" in a text, it is usually a good idea to find out what it is *there for*. Paul has just described the humility and exaltation of Jesus, and then tells us, "Therefore . . . work out your own salvation with fear and trembling." The "therefore" tells us that what Paul is *about* to say is tied to what he *just* said. So, having seen Jesus' example of a life lived in meekness and submission to the Father, we are to respond by "working out our salvation with fear and trembling." Since Jesus took care of salvation at the cross, and since we can add nothing to what He has already done, when Paul says to "work out" our salvation, he is obviously not telling us to accomplish or achieve anything. A better translation might be to "walk out" our salvation. Paul is talking about how we, having been saved, should conduct ourselves. He indicates that we should do it "with fear and trembling." While I'm not sure exactly what that looks like, one thing is certain: we are not to take "working out our salvation" lightly or casually.

Although there is probably a great deal that goes into "working out our salvation with fear and trembling," Paul gives us just a couple of practical insights in the verses that follow. For me, there are few things more frustrating than sitting through a message or sermon without any practical application. However, in this case, a part of me wishes Paul had left this discussion on a "spiritual level." His words here are difficult. He tells us that part of walking out the salvation we have received is to "do all things without complaining or disputing." Ouch.

Loving God with all of my soul, which is evidenced by embracing meekness, is costly. It requires that I die to myself and abandon my "right" to complain when I am mistreated or face difficult circumstances—or difficult people. Paul says we are to avoid complaining, which seems to relate to our circumstances. He tells us we are to avoid disputing, which certainly relates to our interactions with others. This is where the proverbial rubber hits the road. For some of us, like myself, this may seem almost impossible. However, embracing this type of meekness is part of the process by which the Holy Spirit makes us "blameless . . . children of God."

So there it is. There really is no gray area here. Complaining: bad. Disputing: bad. Since both are deeply rooted in our sinful nature, what are we to do? Thankfully, Paul gives some direction. He tells us in verse 16 that our only hope for walking as Jesus walked is to "hold fast the word of life." Paul's prescription for living restrained in our speech is to embrace the Word of the Lord, choosing to speak and agree with the truth of the Scriptures instead of our own careless ramblings. This is not easy. In fact, for most of us it is a constant battle, one where ground is gained and lost on a consistent basis. However, bringing our speech under the leadership of the Holy Spirit and the written Word releases a supernatural work in our heart to produce meekness and humility over time.

In Ephesians 4:29, Paul instructs us to "Let no corrupt word proceed out of [our] mouth[s], but what is good for necessary edification, that it may impart grace to the hearers." This directive has obvious implications with regard to our impact upon the lives of those with whom we come in contact, but there is a personal dimension as well. Since there is no voice that we listen to more intently than our own, the words we speak, more than anyone else's, affect the condition of our own spirit. Our words affect others, and they affect our own inner man. More importantly, they affect the Spirit of God that is at work within

ACCORDING TO PAUL, WHAT WE SAY CAN EITHER ENHANCE OR QUENCH THE MINISTRY OF THE HOLY SPIRIT IN OUR LIVES.

us. After Paul instructs believers to avoid "corrupt" words, he continues (verse 30) by saying, "Do not grieve the Spirit of God." Consequently, according to Paul, what we say can either enhance or quench the ministry of the Holy Spirit in our lives. If that is true, then what we say either increases or diminishes our ability to love God by the power of God, since it is the Spirit of God that provides that power within us.

Let me be clear: unrestrained speech does not affect God's love for us. He is not grieved in the same way that we are grieved. His love is not conditional according to whether we "hurt His feelings." However, our words do affect the degree to which we walk in power.

It is not only true that the words we allow out of our mouths are expressions of the degree to which we are growing in love for God (loving Him with all of our soul), but we also see that setting our hearts to control our tongues is one of the primary keys to expanding our capacity to love. This is a critical reality, and if I'm honest, a somewhat scary one. Even though Paul has given clear direction that the way we avoid complaining and disputing is to embrace and agree with the Word of God, actually doing that can be a struggle. Sometimes it feels a lot like dying. But I have found a way to make the process a little more bearable. I have discovered the secret that makes saying yes to meekness consistently over time a real possibility. It is by not only holding fast to the written Word, but also holding fast to the Word made flesh. As I fix my eyes on Jesus, I am deeply moved by His humility and the way He treats us in our brokenness and immaturity. As I behold Him, I can't help but want to become like Him. Experiencing His love changes my desires and causes me to yearn to submit to the Holy Spirit's process for helping me love Him in return—even when it is costly.

As we set our hearts to allow the Holy Spirit to bring forth humility in our lives, it is important to understand that humility is not just something we endure until we finally get to Heaven, it is the way of God forever, and it will be our way forever. The good news is that while it may be a struggle for us on this side of Heaven, the writer of Hebrews tells us that we are at the same time *perfect* and *being made perfect*. The Holy Spirit will complete the work He has started in our hearts, and in the fullness of time we will become like Him. So for now we reach for meekness by faith, most of the time feeling the sting of humility rather than the pleasure of being humble. The sting I am referring to, however, is the result of our pride being put to death, so that sting is to be embraced. In the midst of it, we can be strengthened by the knowledge that our Father takes great pleasure in our choice.

Chapter Seven

LOVING GOD WITH ALL OUR STRENGTH

"No man gives anything acceptable to God until he has first
given himself in love and sacrifice."

– A.W. Tozer, *That Incredible Christian: How Heaven's
Children Live on Earth*[11]

At the time of this writing, I have been a follower of Jesus for
just short of twenty-four years. In that time, I have listened to
innumerable sermons and read countless books focused on
Jesus' great love for us. This is such a critical topic to discuss
within the church, and quite honestly, it is a reality that none
of us are able to grasp in its entirety. We don't have the capacity. We need to be reminded of the reality of God's love on

---

[11] A.W. Tozer, *That Incredible Christian: How Heaven's Children Live on Earth*
(Camp Hill, PA: Wing Spread Publishers, 1964).

a repetitive basis. The whole gospel boils down to a Savior-God who loves us so radically that He became flesh in order to die a gruesome death and bridge a gap we could not cross. A Bridegroom God who loves us so passionately that He makes known to us His deepest secrets, including His plan for an anticipated return in which He will marry us and make us His own for eternity. A Warrior-King God who loves us so humbly that He will ultimately subdue all things under His feet and invite us to reign with Him in His earthly kingdom. In short, the gospel boils down to a God who loves radically, passionately, and humbly—and then invites us to do the same.

While I am grateful for any message that calls me to greater abandonment and love for Jesus, I think it is important that such exhortations give some substance to how loving God actually plays out in the actions and lifestyle of a believer. At the same time, we must be careful not to err on the side of a works-based love that ultimately leads to legalism and empty religion. This is a delicate and difficult balance. To provide no definition at all can easily leave "loving" God on par with "loving" pizza, meaning that we simply have a strong affinity for that which is "loved." At the same time, equating "loving God" with a to-do list is a surefire path to burnout and misery.

EQUATING "LOVING GOD" WITH A TO-DO LIST IS A SUREFIRE PATH TO BURNOUT AND MISERY.

As we have already discussed, when Jesus was asked about the most important commandment in the Law, he responded by saying that we are to love God with all that we are—heart, soul, mind, and strength. We have examined the first three arenas, and in this chapter I want to dig into the fourth: loving God with all our strength. But before we begin, I feel compelled to offer a word of warning. As we will see, loving God with all our strength has much to do with actions such as serving, giving, and so on. Because of this, it is easy to reduce loving God with all our strength to some sort of "holy checklist" (which, in fact, is not holy at all). We can easily slip into reducing love to moralism or good citizenship, or possibly worse yet, believing that we must be legitimate lovers of God because we have checked all the boxes.

As we saw with Martha, serving is good, but it can become a distraction if done primarily *for* God rather than *with* God. Fasting and prayer are essential, but as we see in Jesus' interaction with the Pharisees, engaging in spiritual disciplines in an attempt to impress or earn anything from God is actually offensive to the Lord. Any outward expression of love by an individual whose heart is devoid of that which they hope to express is nothing more than "sounding brass or a clanging cymbal" (1 Corinthians 13:1). It is showy. It is annoying. In time, it becomes offensive. And, according to the Apostle Paul, it profits us nothing.

So, as we delve into what it looks like to love God with all of our strength, let us be careful to avoid the extremes. Some of us are so afraid of slipping into legalism that we are tempted to totally dismiss setting our hearts and disciplining our bodies to love God with all of our strength. When we do this, we miss out on what Jesus refers to as a critical sphere of loving God with all that we are. If we want to truly see our hearts grow in love and experience the fullness of relationship with the Holy Spirit, we must do it His way, and His way includes loving God with all of our strength. However, lest our fears be realized and we reduce a beautiful encounter to a laundry basket filled with filthy rags, beware of approaching the things we discuss in this chapter as simply ways to prove your love to God (or anyone else, including yourself) or to earn His favor. Instead, consider them a pathway to the bonfire of God's love, by which our frozen hearts are set free and allowed to come alive. Think of them as catalysts that drastically accelerate the Holy Spirit's process of bringing about extravagant lovers of God. The work is His, but we can determine the pace. Realizing that the time is short, why waste any?

The Fasted Lifestyle: Voluntary Weakness

Loving God with all of our strength is synonymous with loving Him with all of our resources. For many of us, when we hear the phrase "loving God with our resources," our minds automatically drift to the last guilt train we were invited to board that was headed down the if-you-truly-love-God-you-will-give-us-your-money track. Well, if you are one of those people, I have some good news and some bad news. First, the good news: I'm not just talking about money, and I don't think Jesus was either. Now, the bad news: I'm not just talking about money, and I don't think Jesus was either. OK, in reality it's actually all good news, as we will see in this chapter.

Let's be clear: God doesn't *need* anything from us. Although He does ask us to lay down everything to follow Him, it is not because He lacks something and our resources can somehow make up the difference. Our time, money, words, food, energy, and influence add nothing to Him, yet He invites us to voluntarily sacrifice and embrace weakness in all of these areas so we can grow in love and experience His heart in full bridal partnership. This is the beautiful, dynamic reality that we will refer to as the "fasted lifestyle."

Unfortunately, fasting is not a popular word in many Christian circles, but I believe the Lord will restore our passion for this experience in the days to come. For those of us who like to eat, just the word itself—fasting—sparks an emotional response that is comparable to a swift kick to the gut. Why? Because, for many of us, food has unwittingly become a god. As silly as it sounds, the god of steak and potatoes has crowded out the God who hand delivers manna and quail. But lest those of you who are not tempted to bow down at the altar of culinary delight develop a prideful spirit, let me be clear: anything that holds our attention and affections in such a tight grip that the thought of going without it causes a gut-wrenching response has been allowed to occupy a position it does not deserve.

IT IS NOT JUST SOME OPTIONAL BEHAVIOR THAT IS ENGAGED IN ONLY BY "RADICAL CHRISTIANS." FOR JESUS, FASTING IS A GIVEN.

While fasting certainly includes passing on food, it ultimately involves embracing voluntary weakness in any area of natural strength and putting to death the temptation to find fulfillment outside of encountering Jesus. We must understand this reality in order for fasting to make sense. The normal use of our strength is to increase our own comfort, wealth, and honor. Through the fasted lifestyle, we bring those natural strengths to God as we express our love for Him, trusting Him to return our strength to us in a way that not only blesses our circumstances, but transforms our heart as well.

While it may seem like it at times, God does not call us to embrace the fasted lifestyle just to see if we will really go after the "hard stuff." Fasting is actually Christianity 101. Jesus did not separate it from what most of us would consider to be the "basics" of the faith: prayer, reading and meditating on the Scriptures, and so on. It is not just some optional behavior that is engaged in only by "radical Christians." For Jesus, fasting is a given. That is why, in the Sermon on the Mount, Jesus tells His followers, "Moreover, *when you fast*, do not be like the hypocrites, with a sad countenance. . . . But you, *when you fast*, anoint your head and wash your face, so that you do not appear to men to be fasting" (Matthew 6:16-18, *emphasis mine*). *When* you fast. Not *if* you fast. Really, Jesus?

So why would Jesus ask us to perform such a "radical" action as embracing the fasted lifestyle? Why would He want us to experience physical weakness by giving up food? Doesn't He know that makes it more difficult for us to get things done? And what good does it possibly do to give our money to a God who uses gold for concrete? Does He really need it? Furthermore, how helpful can it possibly be for us to sit alone in a room, telling God what He tells us to tell Him (prayer), when we could be out serving the poor and changing the world? Embracing weakness goes against conventional wisdom when we consider what is necessary to see God's kingdom established on earth. However, in God's upside-down kingdom, strength is found in weakness and change is often found in waiting. The fasted lifestyle forces us to rely on Him. As our own strength and resources are diminished, we have nowhere to turn but His!

As you probably know, God is not interested primarily in what we can accomplish for Him. His primary concern is that our hearts are growing in love—love for Him and love for those around us. Because God is the Creator and architect of the human spirit, He knows that there are certain social, psychological, emotional, and spiritual dynamics that unfold when we pursue the fasted lifestyle, dynamics that cannot be tapped any other way. Embracing the fasted lifestyle not only expresses our love for God, it also positions us to receive the Spirit's power to love Him more! Our capacity to love is enhanced significantly as we engage with the Holy Spirit in the place of voluntary weakness, trusting God as the source of our strength rather than seeking the rewards of this life. Our hearts are made tender and our motives are revealed, allowing us to cry out for even more of His presence and to experience the gift of repentance more fully.

The fasted lifestyle is one of the foundational dichotomies

of Scripture. God has made something so simple, such as praying and not eating, a source of great power for believers. But oh, how difficult the simple can be! This is especially true when there is a time delay in the return we receive for our efforts. Yet it is in the delay that the God-designed dynamics of the human heart unfold. It is in pushing through the challenges of embracing weakness that our trust in and love for God is revealed.

God's heart is moved at the deepest levels when we trust Him even when our flesh screams of our craziness—when we place encountering God's heart above our natural inclinations. Will we trust the God who seems to have little to no concern for our timelines? Will we choose a heart with an enlarged capacity to love over a comfortable existence? Will we allow love to dictate how we use our resources? Will we submit our will to the invisible God with the delay factor, or allow our lives to be driven by the very visible and urgent task or opportunity? These are difficult questions we must consider. Fasting is by no means a way to earn our way to Heaven, and the Spirit will help us whether we fast or not. But for those who are serious about experiencing intimacy to the fullest degree possible, the simple act of embracing weakness, even when it is difficult, is a catalyst that speeds the growth, like nothing else, of the heart's capacity to love.

The anointing to love God in fullness is the greatest possession the human spirit can attain—the supernatural empowering to feel God's love and love Him in return. If we walk in the anointing to be loyal in love to Jesus, then we have *everything*, and the Holy Spirit releases this anoint-

FATHER, GIVE US GRACE FOR FASTING! THERE ARE SO MANY REWARDS THAT COME WITH LOVING GOD IN THIS WAY THAT IT IS WORTH THE STRUGGLE AND INCONVENIENCE IT ENTAILS.

ing in greater measure as we reach to love God in the way the Scriptures describe. The grace of fasting and embracing voluntary weakness is God's gift to us, as it provides a very practical way of posturing our hearts to experience God's love and the power to love in return. Ask Him for it. Father, give us grace for fasting! There are so many rewards that come with loving God in this way that it is worth the struggle and inconvenience it entails. So many blessings that God desires to pour out on us are given according to our hunger for Him, and there is no catalyst like the fasted lifestyle to boost spiritual hunger. Of course, the greatest of these blessings is an expanded heart with the capacity to love Him even more!

Five Expressions of the Fasted Lifestyle

In Matthew 6, Jesus teaches us five very specific ways in which we are invited to embrace the fasted lifestyle—giving, serving, praying, blessing our enemies, and, of course, fasting. As we have discussed, each of these entail sacrificing physical strength and resources in order to gain ground more quickly in our intimacy with Jesus. Because each flies in the face of what most of us consider "normal" behavior, they are all difficult, at least at first. However, as we examine the Scriptures, we find that all five of these expressions are modeled for us by the greatest men in history, men like Moses, Elijah, John the Baptist, and Paul. These men had a dynamic relationship with God that few have experienced, and each willingly embraced the fasted lifestyle as part of their day-to-day lives.

John the Baptist is perhaps the ultimate expression of what it looks like to love God with all our strength—at least when it comes to a man who is not also fully God. His regular diet consisted of locusts and wild honey. He had no regard whatsoever for his reputation, spending his life being viewed by most as a lonely desert wanderer who was a few fries short of a

Happy Meal. His ministry lasted only about eighteen months, and relatively speaking, the number of people who came to his "worship services" was miniscule. By today's standards, John's ministry would likely be considered a complete failure. However, Jesus had a different opinion. When He spoke about John, Jesus said, "Assuredly, I say to you, among those born of women there has not risen one greater than John the Baptist" (Matthew 11:11). Pretty good endorsement for a ministry failure, yes?

Speaking of Jesus, how about a quick glimpse at what it looks like for God to love God with all of His strength?! Jesus is both fully man and fully God, yet He made it His life's work to make much of His Father. He fasted. He served. He gave. He prayed. He blessed His enemies—even after they nailed Him to a Roman cross. As God, Jesus has all power, but as man, He laid it all down out of love for His Father and for us.

> JESUS IS BOTH FULLY MAN AND FULLY GOD, YET HE MADE IT HIS LIFE'S WORK TO MAKE MUCH OF HIS FATHER.

What's more, it did not end at the cross: "Then comes the end, when [Jesus] delivers the kingdom to God the Father . . . when all things are made subject to [Jesus], then the Son Himself will also be subject to [the Father] who put all things under [the Son], that God may be all in all" (1 Corinthians 15:24-28). When Jesus returns to the earth, the Scriptures tell us, He will rule as an earthly King for a period of one thousand years. During that time, all things will be under His control. He will have ultimate strength in every area of life. He will rule every nation; every knee will bow, and every tongue will confess that He is Lord. However, according to that Scripture, at the end of that earthly reign, Jesus will lay it all down once again, delivering every nation to God the Father and subjecting Himself in love. What an incredible expression!

So, as we can see, by inviting us to embrace the fasted life-style, Jesus is really inviting us to enter in to the fellowship of love that has existed since before time began. While it is a struggle at times, laying down our strength in the five areas that Jesus outlines in Matthew 6 is actually a very small price to pay. The reward far outweighs the price! In giving up food, we fast our physical and emotional strength. In giving, we fast our money, our financial strength. In serving and prayer, we fast our time and energy by investing it in seeking God and helping others. In blessing our enemies, we fast our words and reputation. Is it difficult to do these things consistently? You bet it is! But we do them anyway, as an expression of love for Jesus and as a means to position ourselves to receive power to love Him more. It all comes down to what we *truly* value.

Fasting: Loving God with Our Physical and Mental Strength

Most of us immediately think of giving up a few meals when we hear a phrase like "the fasted lifestyle." This is certainly one aspect or expression we need to incorporate into our lives, but for many of the Christ-followers whom I know, it is conspicuously absent. Of course, there are some who have health conditions that make fasting dangerous or even life-threatening. However, I would wager that most of us have not even given the idea serious consideration.

On the other hand, for those who have taken the plunge into fasting, many have done so somewhat begrudgingly. Why? Simple. *Because it is hard!* It is especially difficult for most Westerners. We like to eat. Most of us get irritable when our meal schedule is slightly delayed, let alone completely disrupted. I admit this is a struggle for me, but as I have begun to learn the dynamics of what is actually taking place—viewing giving up food as an expression of love and a source of power—it has certainly become easier to embrace. I think this is because it is really the fear of fasting that is worse than fasting itself! However, as John tells us in 1 John 4:18, "perfect love casts out fear," so viewing fasting through the lens of a lover who is deeply loved makes it significantly easier. In fact, of all the expressions of the fasted lifestyle than Jesus outlines, this is probably the easiest. Blessing my enemies, not so much. But we will talk about that shortly.

One of the issues that always made giving up food difficult for me (other than the obvious hunger element) was not being able to understand what difference it could possibly make. I have always been an expert in the dynamics of how eating can enlarge my gut, but for years it was completely unclear to me how *not* eating could enlarge my capacity to love. I think I am finally beginning to get at least a little bit of understanding. When we are presented with a physical craving, it takes little effort for us to embrace that awareness and take steps to address or resolve it. When our stomach growls, we eat. Sadly, our spirit groans within us constantly, and many times we are completely oblivious. Now, there is nothing wrong with eating—try stopping altogether and see how that works for you. However, when we overindulge in even the most legitimate physical appetites, this is typically accompanied by a quenching of the Spirit's life within us.

The reality is that even healthy, God-given pleasures will dull our spirits if they are allowed to reach a point of excess. So, while it is certainly not wrong to eat, it is dangerous to allow any pleasure to become more important or satisfying to us than God's presence. Addressing this requires that we often deny ourselves legitimate pleasures that are not sinful in themselves, but also do not serve to enhance our sensitivity to the Spirit of God. Often, we will find that our hunger for the things of God increases significantly when we do not quench that hunger with food, recreation, money, or other pursuits.

In addition to the overindulgence concern, there is also the issue of embracing weakness so God can display His strength. While hunger is certainly a reality that comes with fasting, abstaining from food is really more about embracing physical and mental weakness than it is about being hungry. When we sacrifice our physical strength and mental acuteness to God, it will cause us to experience blurry thinking, a weak body, a foggy memory, and a decreased ability to communicate. We may even miss opportunities for personal success in a number of areas. It requires us to lean on God for strength in even the most basic areas of life and trust Him to give back to us in the areas in which we have sacrificed. Sometimes that return gift is directly related to that which we have given up, and sometimes it is simply the grace to be more in tune with His Spirit. Whatever the case, what we receive in return far surpasses that which we have sacrificed—a person simply cannot out-give God!

Giving Money: Loving God with Our Financial Strength

In a world that so deeply values acquiring wealth and "keeping up with the Joneses," our financial resources are certainly a significant element of our societal strength and influence. I admit, as a follower of Jesus, I am still struggling to nail down a consistent theology of the appropriate role of finances in the life of a believer. Money gets a bad rap in many Christian circles, and it is seen as a sign of great faith and holiness in others. However, as best I can tell, in and of itself, money is neither inherently good nor evil. But one thing is abundantly clear: the *love of money* is deadly. In fact, Jesus said it is *impossible* to love both God and money: "Do not lay up for yourselves treasures on earth . . . but lay up for yourselves treasures in heaven . . . For where your treasure is, there your heart will be also. . . . No one can serve two masters; for either he will hate the one and love the other, or else he will be loyal to the one and despise the other. You cannot serve God and [money]" (Matthew 6:19-24).

According to Jesus, wherever we invest our "treasure," which is not only our money, but certainly includes it, that is where our heart will be inspired. Our emotions and affections are dynamically connected to that in which we choose to invest our finances and other treasures. When we give our money away in order to build God's kingdom on the earth, we are declaring our refusal to allow our heart to be driven by earthly dynamics. We are expressing our commitment to keeping our affections squarely set on Jesus and what is most important to Him. When we voluntarily embrace weakness in this area (and others), trusting Jesus to be our primary source in all things, He counts it as an expression of love, and it touches His heart on the deepest level. Not only that, but when we pour our treasure into God in the ways He describes, it impacts *our* hearts as well! We must not be deceived into believing that we can live like everyone else in how we invest our resources and wake up one day with an expanded heart with a greater capacity to love. It simply won't happen. Conversely, if we make Him our treasure, our destiny as fully devoted lovers is secure.

When we talk about giving money, one question that typ-

> WE MUST NOT BE DECEIVED INTO BELIEVING THAT WE CAN LIVE LIKE EVERYONE ELSE IN HOW WE INVEST OUR RESOURCES AND WAKE UP ONE DAY WITH AN EXPANDED HEART WITH A GREATER CAPACITY TO LOVE. IT SIMPLY WON'T HAPPEN.

ically comes to mind is, "How much?" Well, it is probably important to first clarify that God does not need our money. He uses gold for concrete, so our checking account is neither impressive to Him nor essential to His purposes. God is not after our money, but our hearts. So, really, our question should not be "How much *should* I give?" but rather, "How much *can* I give? How abandoned can I really be in my pursuit of knowing and encountering Jesus?" In an earlier chapter we discussed Mary of Bethany and her costly sacrifice, pouring perfume that was worth a year's wages on Jesus' feet. She was obviously not concerned with the minimum amount she could give and still remain in Jesus' good graces. She gave *everything* she had. That should be our aim as well.

Since I live in the realm of reality and realize that almost none of us are at the "Mary of Bethany level" yet, let's discuss a couple of practical guidelines to keep in mind as we seek to love God through our giving. First, the amount is not important. The widow who gave her last two mites (small copper coins) showed much more love for God than those who gave more money yet sacrificed less. When Jesus saw her contribution, He said, "Truly I say to you that this poor widow has put in more than all; for all these out of their abundance have put in offerings for God, but she out of her poverty put in all the livelihood that she had" (Luke 21:2-4). It is not the amount that concerns God, but the costliness of the sacrifice. Which brings us to the second point.

In order for our giving to truly be an expression of love for Jesus, it must force us to wrestle with the emotional dynamics associated with covetousness and the fear of lack. So, in short, give until it hurts! Give until you feel it significantly. Again, it is not the amount that matters, but the sacrifice. King David had set his heart to live radically by loving God with his money, and as a result, he refused to give anything to God that did not cost him in a significant way. When God told David to build Him an altar on the threshing floor of Araunah the Jebusite, Araunah was so honored that the king had come to him that he offered to give the threshing floor to David at no cost. However, David responded to Araunah by saying, "No, but I will surely buy it from you at a price; nor will I offer burnt offerings to the Lord my God with that which costs me nothing" (2 Samuel 24:24). And David kept his commitment in a big way. Not only did he purchase the threshing floor from Araunah, but when it came time to build the Temple, David gave more than one hundred billion dollars (in today's prices) from his personal finances!

In 1 Chronicles 29:3, David says to the assembly that had gathered, "Moreover, because I have set my affection on the house of my God, I have given to the house of my God, over and above all that I have prepared for the holy house, my own special treasure of gold and silver." David set his affections on God, and therefore was willing to sacrifice much to see the Temple become a reality. Because he had developed a history of giving sacrificially, He was not held back from loving God extravagantly with his finances due to some unconquered dynamic hidden in his heart. It may take a lot of little steps for us to get to that point, but it sure sounds like a pretty liberating way to live!

One more quick consideration before we move on. God's work in our heart as a result of our giving is drastically minimized if we are getting all of the kudos for what we have done. That is why Jesus tells us that when we give, we should be careful to "not let [our] left hand know what [our] right hand is doing" (Matthew 6:3). That is not to say that our giving is in vain if someone finds out and says "thank you." The important issue here is that we remember that the focus of our giving should be on encountering Jesus in fullness and not "getting ahead" with man. This is certainly a real temptation, and one that can be easily justified in our minds. But Jesus says to be careful about it. Let's assume His instruction trumps our justification.

Serving Others: Loving God with Our Strength in Time and Energy

I think most followers of Jesus understand the importance of helping and serving others, but if my life is any indication, the reality is few of us actually do it on a regular basis. I don't think this is because we don't want to. Most of us do. But we are busy. Very busy. And because we are so busy, most of us are fairly limited in the energy department as well. How often do we find ourselves aware of a need or opportunity where we could help, yet utter the phrase, "I just don't have the time"? I would love to show you a verse that would give credence to our claim and allow us to justify our behavior, a place in Scripture where Jesus tells us to serve as long as we can fit it in our schedules, but, well . . . I can't.

In serving others, we choose to invest our time and energy, assets that could be used to further our own interests, in God's purposes and kingdom. Time that we might otherwise use for earning income, networking, socializing, or being entertained is poured out on others as an expression of love for both Jesus and the ones we serve. But as with other areas in which we choose to embrace the fasted lifestyle, the rewards far outweigh the sacrifice.

Time and energy are valuable resources, potentially the most valuable ones at our disposal. Yet as we give them away freely, choosing to put God's agenda above our own, we show love for Jesus and position our hearts to be expanded to love even more. More importantly, it is in serving others that we come face to face with the Servant of all. His deepest desire is that we would encounter Him where He is, and what better place to find the ultimate Servant than in the act of serving!

I can think of no better way to make my life count, in this age and the next, than to partner with Jesus by loving and serving others, understanding all the while that He takes that service personally, and it moves His heart.

As we seek to develop a lifestyle in which we honor and love Jesus through our service, let us remember that it is just that: a lifestyle. In other words, don't just wait for the next "church outreach." While there is certainly value in participating in scheduled projects with others in the body, it is easy to fall into the trap of checking off service projects on our "spiritual checklist" and then not thinking about it again until the next formal opportunity arises. As followers of Jesus who truly desire to have our hearts expanded in love, let us commit to looking for opportunities to serve regularly. Check in on the elderly neighbor. Spend some time talking with her. Ask what you can do to help. Make a regular time in your schedule to serve at the homeless shelter or soup kitchen. Take your family along. Teach your kids what it looks like to live a life of service.

Speaking of your family, service is by no means limited to our interactions with the homeless and hungry. While we are commanded to care for those who are less fortunate, those opportunities are not always in front of us. Focus on serving the ones you live with. Let's face it, once we make the difficult adjustments to carve out the time that is necessary, most of us can get excited about the big service opportunities. On the other hand, it is not always easy to get fired up about serving your spouse and children. Do it anyway. Be intentional. I assure you, you won't regret it.

Prayer: Loving God with Our Time and Emotional Strength

Prayer and reading the Word (the two, in truth, are inseparable) are a form of weakness in which we sacrifice both our time and emotional strength. As with giving of our time in serving, when we pray we pass up opportunities to advance our own agendas through networking, socializing, or being entertained. Instead of using our time to seek comfort and success, we choose to talk to an invisible God, telling Him what He tells us to tell Him and waiting patiently (sometimes) for His response, which is often delayed. In doing this, we entrust ourselves to the Lord for our promotion and provision. While the investment may seem costly at times, the truth is that we can never lose a single minute we have given to God in the place of prayer—and we can't recover a single minute that we didn't.

In addition to making a time sacrifice, prayer also requires that we embrace weakness in the area of our emotions. When we move beyond the simple "bless me" prayers (there is nothing wrong with those, by the way) to true intercession, it takes a certain amount of emotional energy. To really engage with the Lord requires that we truly pour ourselves out before Him, moving well beyond simply rattling off our standard lines for a few minutes at meals or before bed. As we do this, we position our cold hearts before the bonfire of God's grace, and we receive empowering from the Holy Spirit to grow in love.

> AS WE GROW IN GRACE FOR PRAYER, WE EXPERIENCE GREATER INTIMACY TODAY, AND WE ARE PROMISED SUPERNATURAL COURAGE AND DIRECTION AT THE END OF THE AGE.

The church *must* rediscover the lost art of giving of ourselves in the area of prayer! The exhortation that Jesus gave most often to help us prepare for the end of the age is to "watch and pray," to develop a heart connection with the Spirit in the place of prayer. Jesus lovingly warns His disciples in Mark 13:33, "Take heed, watch and pray; for you do not know when the time is." We cannot know the time of His return, but we can know His heart, and we can ensure that we are ready when He does return! There is no better investment we can make than to develop a vibrant prayer life. As we grow in grace for prayer, we experience greater intimacy today, and we are promised supernatural courage and direction at the end of the age.

Forgiveness of and Blessing Enemies: Loving God with Our Social Strength

OK, now for the most difficult one on the list, at least for me. I like to eat, I can be pretty stingy and self-serving, and I often struggle to engage in prayer, but none of those shortcomings compare with my fiery temper and thirst for revenge when someone mistreats or talks badly about me. It's bad. Really bad. I can come up with some pretty good justifications in most cases! However, Jesus disarms even the most "airtight" case with one simple statement regarding the way of the kingdom: "For if you forgive men their trespasses, your heavenly Father will also forgive you" (Matthew 6:14). I may not be the brightest bulb in the sign, but it doesn't take me long to discern the implied corollary: if we don't forgive others, *then God will not forgive us.*

Wait a minute! I thought my works were insignificant when it comes to forgiveness! How can my forgiveness be contingent upon offering the same to others? Good question. God is filled with mercy, and He longs to forgive, but Jesus seems to be making a critical point here. Since it is not the primary focus of this book, I will leave you to wrestle with it on your own. Sorry about that. But not really.

Then, as if Jesus' difficult teaching on the importance of forgiveness is not enough, He takes it a step further: "[L]ove your enemies, bless those who curse you" (Matthew 5:44). For

Jesus, forgiveness is only the beginning. It is the doorway by which we are then able to love and bless those who have hurt us. When we forgive, we reflect the character of Jesus Himself: "[W]hen He was reviled, did not revile in return; when He suffered, He did not threaten, but committed Himself to Him who judges righteously" (1 Peter 2:23). When Jesus was mistreated, He forgave and blessed. He did not fight back. Instead, He entrusted Himself to His Father's care.

When we forgive and then bless our enemies, it requires us to embrace weakness in the area of our words, relationships, and reputation. To actively bless our enemies means to refrain from using our words to justify our positions, expose those who have hurt or slandered us, or gain the sympathy and support of others. Granted, there are times when it is certainly legitimate, and even necessary, to expose injustice and wrongdoing, such as in the case of abuse or exploitation. However, at least in the majority of cases, the wrongs committed against us are far less severe.

Instead of using our strength to defend and promote ourselves, the Lord calls us to restrain our speech, and He counts it as love when we do. He is touched when we choose obedience and find both identity and comfort in simply knowing Him. Sure, we give up some of the social strength we might gain or maintain from fighting back, but our hearts are expanded. In silence, we commit ourselves to God to vindicate us, displaying to our Father and to the world that our trust truly is in Him.

The Rewards of Fasting

Although I have mentioned this several times already, it bears repeating: the rewards of fasting far outweigh the sacrifice. Really, there is no comparison. The Father rewards fasting in a number of ways:

- Internally—our capacity to love is expanded and our sensitivity to an encounter with the Holy Spirit is increased

- Externally—fasting is often accompanied by a blessing on our circumstances

- Eternally—we give up treasure on earth in order to lay up for ourselves treasure in Heaven

All three of these areas of blessing are legitimate and important, but since the focus of this book is on growing in love for Jesus, I want to end this chapter with just a few comments regarding the internal rewards that fasting brings.

Fasting makes our hearts more tender and sensitive over time and allows us to receive grace to love Jesus more. There is something about the fasted lifestyle that allows us to love Jesus with increased focus, consistency, and intensity, which is accompanied by an increased zeal for righteousness. As we combine fasting with prayer, we are positioned to receive deliverance from various sinful addictions that keep us from feeling God's love and believing that our love for Him is legitimate. Isaiah exhorts us to fast in order to "loose the bonds of wickedness" (Isaiah 58:6) so we might be freed from sinful behaviors. While the context of Isaiah's exhortation is specifically in regard to oppressing the less fortunate, the "bonds of wickedness" that are loosed through fasting include other common sins like bondage to pornography, immorality, anger, alcohol/drug abuse, gluttony, and greed, to name only a few.

In addition to experiencing freedom from the entangling sins that hold us back from loving Jesus fully, fasting also brings freedom from the circumstances that so easily distract us from growing in love. While fasting by no means causes our problems to disappear, it does allow us to gain divine perspective as we become more preoccupied with loving Jesus than we are with worry, fear, and needless striving. As the Holy Spirit reveals God's "big picture" and the life that awaits us in eternity, this one suddenly seems bearable. More importantly, disentanglement from the affairs of this life allows us to begin living now as we will in the life to come—enthralled with Jesus and in full bridal partnership with the Lover of our souls.

Chapter Eight

POSITIONING OUR HEARTS

"Let your heart and mind be kept close to the principal calling of your life, which is to hunger and thirst after God and His righteousness. . . . Let the thoughts and intents of your heart be shaped and guided by time spent in His presence."

– Ravi Zacharias, *I, Isaac, Take Thee, Rebekah: Moving from Romance to Lasting Love*[12]

While I find many of Jesus' parables in the Gospels to be a little challenging to fully grasp, I believe the story He shares in Mark 4 conveys a message that is crystal clear and critically important for every believer to understand: Growing in love for God does not happen automatically or without intentionality. Since everyone who is reading this may not be familiar with the passage, let's look at it briefly.

---

[12] Ravi Zacharias, *I, Isaac, Take Thee, Rebekah: Moving from Romance to Lasting Love* (Nashville: Thomas Nelson, 2004), 121.

And again [Jesus] began to teach by the sea. And a great multitude was gathered to Him, so that He got into a boat and sat in it on the sea; and the whole multitude was on the land facing the sea. Then He taught them many things by parables, and said to them in His teaching:

"Listen! Behold, a sower went out to sow. And it happened, as he sowed, that some seed fell by the wayside; and the birds of the air came and devoured it. Some fell on stony ground, where it did not have much earth; and immediately it sprang up because it had no depth of earth. But when the sun was up it was scorched, and because it had no root it withered away. And some seed fell among thorns; and the thorns grew up and choked it, and it yielded no crop. But other seed fell on good ground and yielded a crop that sprang up, increased and produced: some thirtyfold, some sixty, and some a hundred."

And He said to them, "He who has ears to hear, let him hear!" (Mark 4:1-9).

Jesus shares this parable with the large crowd, and then, when everyone but his closest disciples has gone away, He provides a detailed explanation of what this story is truly about. It is rare for Jesus to tell a story like this and then immediately follow it up with the interpretation, so it seems clear that what Jesus was teaching here is extremely important to Him, and He wanted to make sure His disciples couldn't possibly miss it. Since we don't want to miss it either, let's take a quick look.

The sower sows the word. And these are the ones by the wayside where the word is sown. When they hear, Satan comes immediately and takes away the word that was sown in their hearts. These likewise are the ones sown on stony ground who, when they hear the word, immediately receive it with gladness; and they have no root in themselves, and so endure only for a time. Afterward, when tribulation or persecution arises for the word's sake, immediately they stumble. Now these are the ones sown among thorns; they are the ones who hear the word, and the cares of this world, the deceitfulness of riches, and the desires for other things entering in choke the word, and it becomes unfruitful. But these are the ones sown on good ground, those who hear the word, accept it, and bear fruit: some thirtyfold, some sixty, and some a hundred (Mark 4:13-20).

Notice that every time the sower sows seed, it never takes root and produces a crop unless the ground has been prepared. In the same way, the realities of the kingdom of God, including the ability to love God with all of our heart, soul, mind, and strength, cannot be fruitful in our lives unless our hearts are positioned to receive them. God's greatest commandment is to love Him with everything we are, and all of God's commandments include the promise of His enabling us to obey them. The Father will give us a supernatural impartation to love Jesus if we seek after it. The Holy Spirit is eager to help even the weakest of us to grow in love if we ask Him. Nevertheless, we must be intentional in our seeking and asking. Love for God never comes automatically. The truth is that our hearts are always either growing or shrinking. When it comes to the first and greatest commandment, there is no such thing as standing still. We must actively cultivate a responsive heart!

So how do we cultivate this kind of heart? Great question! The means by which we grow in love for God is really not mysterious. In fact, it is actually quite simple. Don't get me wrong, it is extremely costly, but it is not confusing or difficult to grasp. It is a shame that so many of us waste years reaching and groping in the dark for some sort of secret formula or process when God has actually made it so simple. As Moses told the Israelites in Deuteronomy 30:11-14:

> Now what I am commanding you today is not too diffi-cult for you or beyond your reach. It is not up in heaven, so that you have to ask, "Who will ascend into heaven to get it and proclaim it to us so we may obey it?" Nor is it beyond the sea, so that you have to ask, "Who will cross the sea to get it and proclaim it to us so we may obey it?" No, the word is very near you; it is in your mouth and in your heart so you may obey it (NIV).

The problem is not that the truth is beyond our ability to comprehend. Rather, it is that too many of us lack faith in the simple process that God outlines in His Word. There is no such thing as a "quick fix" or overnight success. God has ordained a process that takes years. Decades. A lifetime. We often lack confidence that His process is actually accomplishing what He promised it would, so we are tempted to disconnect from it and seek another way. After years of seeking alternatives and coming up short, I am here to tell you definitively that there is simply no other way. Pray for patience. Fight through the disillusionment. Do whatever you have to do, but don't give up! The core issue for so many sincere believers is that we quit too early because things aren't moving as quickly as we think they should. This is a sad reality, because our Father promises us that we all can make it if we stick to the plan—His plan.

The Oil of Intimacy

In my opinion, the plan God outlined for followers of Jesus to have their hearts expanded in love is best summarized in a series of parables He shares with His disciples in Matthew 24 and 25. In these two chapters, Jesus teaches His disciples about the events surrounding the end of this age. He speaks with them about the Great Tribulation and His Second Coming in order to help believers know what we should expect and how to navigate a period that will be marked by confusion for so many. Jesus then shares three parables to elaborate on His teachings and drive home the importance of being diligent, staying connected to the Holy Spirit, and remaining faithful during the difficult times to come. The majority of Matthew 24 describes what is going to occur, while the final verses of that chapter and the majority of Matthew 25 outline how we are to respond to those events. While the greatest relevance of these teachings is to the generation that will witness the return of Jesus, their truths are certainly applicable to all His followers. Whether Jesus returns in five years, fifty years, or five hundred years, woe to those who overlook the application of His words today!

The first parable that Jesus shares, found in Matthew 24:45-51, describes a situation in which Jesus' delay in returning to the earth is *shorter* than expected. These verses tell the story of two servants who are entrusted with their master's business while he is away. The faithful servant discharges his duties while the master is away, and when master returns, he is pleased with the servant and makes him the "ruler over all his goods." However, the second servant takes advantage of his position of authority, beating his fellow servants and reveling with drunkards. The servant does not expect the master to return quickly, and he is not concerned with being about the master's business while he is away. However, Jesus tells us that "the master of that servant will come on a day when he is not looking for him and at an hour he is not aware of, and will cut him in two and appoint him his portion with the hypocrites" (Matthew 24:50-51). The moral of the story? The

Master expects diligence and integrity from His servants.

The second story in the series focuses on circumstances in which Jesus' delay is *longer* than expected. This is the passage I would like to focus on in this section, because while all three parables are relevant to our pursuit of the first commandment, I believe this one has the most obvious significance. In Matthew 25:1-13, Jesus emphasizes the importance of connecting with the Holy Spirit and cultivating intimacy with Jesus, our Bridegroom King. He exhorts His listeners to "get oil for their lamps," a phrase which carries such deep significance that we *must* not casually dismiss it. We will return to this parable and explore it in more detail momentarily.

Finally, Jesus shares a parable in which His delay is *harder* than expected. In this story, the master of the house leaves for an extended time of travel, and before leaving, he entrusts three of his servants with varying amounts of gold. To one servant he gives five bags, to another he gives two bags, and to a third servant only one. The servant who receives the five bags of gold invests them, and as a result, he gains five more. The servant who receives two bags also makes wise investments, and he is able to gain two additional bags. Both servants are able to not only give the master back the original amounts with which they were entrusted, but they double their money and pay the master with interest. As a result, the master commends them for their faithfulness and invites them to share in his happiness. However, the third servant does not receive the same commendation; he is only able to return the original bag of gold that he was given. Instead of putting the small amount he was given to work while the master is away, he acts in fear, hiding the gold in the ground. The master is angry with the servant, not only condemning his actions but taking away from him the small amount he was given. This story emphasizes the importance of being faithful in our assignment, even when it seems insignificant and difficult.

Again, all three of these parables are vitally important for every believer, but for our purposes in this discussion, I would like to dig in and explore the second in more depth.

"Then the Kingdom of heaven shall be likened to ten virgins who took their lamps and went out to meet the bridegroom. Now five of them were wise, and five were foolish" (Matthew 25:1-2). There are several important facts worth noting in these two verses. First, all ten of the individuals in this story are referred to as virgins. All ten are believers who have been made pure through Jesus' death on the cross and the impartation of his righteousness. We know from the start that this story is not about five righteous folks and five evil ones; rather, it is about five wise and five foolish. Also, each of the virgins carries a lamp when she goes out to meet the Bridegroom. The lamp represents a ministry of some sort through which God's light is shared with those around them. All ten are actively engaged in the mission of seeing the kingdom established on earth. Finally, we are told that each of the ten virgins goes out to "meet the bridegroom." Each has at least some revelation of Jesus as the Bridegroom God. On some level, each has grasped the reality of the ravished heart of God for His bride, the church.

So this story is about ten sincere believers who are actively engaged in ministry and understand, on at least some level, that they are deeply and passionately loved by God. However, there is one point of divergence between the first five and the second five, and it is here that we learn why five are called wise and five labeled foolish. "Those who were foolish took their lamps and took no oil with them, but the wise took oil in their vessels with their lamps" (Matthew 25:3-4). The difference between the wise and foolish virgins is that the wise took oil with their lamps. In the parable, oil represents the presence of the Holy Spirit and our heart connection with Him. We "get oil" by cultivating our secret life in God, and without it, we have no hope of walking out the commandments to love God and love others.

Just like the ten virgins, every believer carries a lamp. Each of us has a ministry to the Lord and those around us. However, if we do not have oil for our lamps, it is only a matter of time before they are extinguished. It is synonymous to putting gas in a car. It doesn't matter how fancy your car is, if you don't stop regularly at the gas station, before long you will be pushing it rather than riding in it. I speak from experience when I tell you that if you push the car for very long, it wears you out. This is true both literally and figuratively. Cars were not made to be pushed, but driven. Ministry was not intended to be our focus or priority, but something that flows naturally out of fellowship with the Holy Spirit. Because ministry is tangible in many ways, it is easy to elevate it to first place. This is especially true when the Lord chooses to bless our ministry and we begin to see it grow. But don't let the blessing of God in one season set you up for failure in the next. Without oil, nothing you do will last. It will all amount to nothing in the end.

> DON'T LET THE BLESSING OF GOD IN ONE SEASON SET YOU UP FOR FAILURE IN THE NEXT.

Just ask the five foolish virgins.

"But while the Bridegroom was delayed, they all slumbered and slept. And at midnight a cry was heard: 'Behold, the Bridegroom is coming, go out to meet him!' Then all those virgins arose and trimmed their lamps" (Matthew 25:5-7). On an initial reading of this verse, it may appear that a major mistake was made by all ten virgins. After all, every one of them is asleep when the Bridegroom appears. However, Jesus says that five of them were wise, so the fact that they all slept is obviously not negative. Instead, in this parable, sleeping speaks of living in context of the natural processes of life. We must sustain our intimacy with Jesus in the midst of the rigors of the routine and mundane. So, again, the problem is not that the ten virgins all slept, but that five did not have the oil necessary to sustain themselves.

The five foolish virgins realized their mistake quickly, but their response further reveals their lack of understanding. "And the foolish said to the wise, 'Give us some of your oil, for our lamps are going out'" (Matthew 25:8). The five wise virgins respond by answering, "No, lest there should not be enough for us and you; but go rather to those who sell, and buy for yourselves" (Matthew 25:9). This may seem harsh at first, but in reality it shows great humility and wisdom on the part of the five wise virgins. They understand their own need for oil and the value it holds while acknowledging their secret history with the Lord and that their spiritual preparedness could not be transferred to others.

My heart's greatest desire is to be counted among the five wise virgins, yet my greatest struggle is slowing down long enough to buy oil. I can identify so well with Paul when he says, "For what I am doing, I do not understand. For what I will to do, that I do not practice; but what I hate, that I do" (Romans 7:15). The fact is that you cannot get oil on the run. You must slow down. Oil is only sold in the secret place. The true oil merchant for our souls abides in the prayer closet, not on the roadside. The first and second commandments are walked out in the rigors of every-day life, and we follow them while on the move, walking out the wisdom imparted to us through the written Word and the leadings of the Holy Spirit. On the contrary, the acquiring of oil occurs in stillness and solitude. It is a statement of humility and a recognition of our inability to even approach loving

> THE FACT IS THAT YOU CANNOT GET OIL ON THE RUN. YOU MUST SLOW DOWN.

God and loving people in a biblical manner without help from the Holy Spirit. It is an affirmation of the words of Jesus in John 15:5: "I am the vine, you are the branches. He who abides in Me, and I in Him, bears much fruit; for without Me you can do nothing."

Relentless Pursuit

Jesus' exhortation to "buy oil" is a call to engage in the God-ordained process of developing intimacy with Him. It is not something we earn, but something we receive when we invest ourselves in a costly way. In the three parables I referenced from Matthew 24 and 25, Jesus tells us twice precisely how we go about acquiring the oil of which He speaks. "Watch therefore, for you do not know what hour your Lord is coming" (Matthew 24:42). "Watch therefore, for you know neither the day nor the hour in which the Son of Man is coming" (Matthew 25:13). Did you catch it? Two of the three parables are followed by the directive to *watch*. However, the watching that Jesus speaks of here is not at all passive. On the contrary, it necessitates action.

We "watch" by actively engaging with the Holy Spirit through studying the Word, prayer, and worship, all while seeking to recognize and respond to the signs of the times and what God is doing in and around us. As I said in the opening paragraphs of this chapter, growing in love for God never comes automatically, but through focused action in response to His great love for us. Our watching must be marked by intentionality and determination, yet so many of us lack an action plan for pursuing the first commandment to grow in passionate love for Jesus. My hope here is to provide at least a few practical thoughts to consider as you map out what it looks like for you to "watch."

First, nothing we do in order to position our hearts to grow in love will amount to anything meaningful if we do not make a long-term, committed decision in our hearts to love God. Our response to His love must begin as a resolute choice to have a heart of affectionate obedience. This sounds so simple, yet I believe it is the reason so many of us live in a state of perpetual dullness. Maybe we hear a great message at church or have a conversation with a friend that stirs our emotions, and we decide once again to try to carve out room in our schedule for Bible study and prayer. Maybe we even follow through for a couple of weeks. But what happens when we begin to feel the pressure of the many demands on our time and we have a few consecutive quiet times during which our emotions are not stirred and the Bible seems a little dull and boring? I won't speak for you, but my track record shows a tendency to stray from what is important in order to address what seems to be most urgent on that particular day.

If we are to truly see our hearts expanded in passionate love for Jesus, we must regularly realign our hearts, intentionally renewing our vision to make loving God our first priority. Our vision must go beyond a general desire to love God and become a specific commitment to centering our lives around loving Him, both today and for the next several decades. While the Holy Spirit is faithful to begin the process, His stirrings do not initiate some sort of "autopilot" that will carry us through to the end. Like King David, we must make the declaration, "I *will* love you, O Lord, my strength" (Psalm 18:1).

Rather than consistently trying to determine what the minimum requirements are in order for us to receive salvation, our focus should shift to asking the question, "What is the most that God will empower me to give Him? How abandoned will He anoint my heart to be?" We must set our hearts to love Him extravagantly, even when we don't feel like it. Sometimes the journey is easy and fascinating, and other times it is costly and boring. Whatever the case, if we resolve in our hearts to be steady in love, God will supernaturally empower us to keep that commitment. The words of the psalmist declare the promise of the Lord to those who make loving Him their first priority: "Because he has set his love upon Me, therefore I will deliver him" (Psalm 91:14).

Having made a commitment to establish growing in love for God as first place on our priority list, it follows that we would then want to seek out and take advantage of every available opportunity to commune with Him in a meaningful way. Of course, one of the primary ways we go about this is through time spent in the Word. I am not talking about just fulfilling a perceived responsibility to have a daily Bible study or "quiet time," but rather engaging in long, lovesick gazing upon the person of Jesus as revealed in the Scriptures. Granted, there are times when our devotions may feel more like acts of pure discipline than something we find enjoyable, but over time, as we continually place our frozen hearts before the fiery eyes of the One who walks among the seven lampstands (Revelation 1:12-14), we begin to feel ourselves come alive in love to a degree we never thought possible.

Revelation of God's love for us equips our hearts to love Jesus, and we can only love Him to the degree that we understand and experience His love for us. This is why the Apostle John tells us that "We love Him *because* He first loved us" (1 John 4:19). But growing in this revelation takes time—we don't get it on the run. We gain revelation by spending hour after hour in the secret place, quietly meditating on God's Word. However, the investment of time is well worth the payoff, as we become able to say, along with "the disciple whom Jesus loved" (John 13:23, NIV): "Behold what manner of love the Father has bestowed on us, that we should be called children of God!" (1 John 3:1).

Of course, even quality time in the Word is only of limited value if we don't use it as a jumping-off point for conversation

QUALITY TIME IN THE WORD IS ONLY OF LIMITED VALUE IF WE DON'T USE IT AS A JUMPING-OFF POINT FOR CONVERSATION WITH THE LORD ABOUT WHAT IS REVEALED TO US.

with the Lord about what is revealed to us. I suggest beginning every interaction with the Scriptures by asking the Holy Spirit to pour out love and revelation into your heart as you read. The Apostle Paul prayed for the believers in Ephesus, asking the Lord to make them able to "comprehend with all the saints what is the width and length and depth and height—to know the love of Christ which passes knowledge" (Ephesians 3:18-19). This is a great model prayer for us to pray as well, both for ourselves and for other followers of Jesus. Too often, when we hear the phrase "the prayer of faith," we immediately think of praying for healing or some sort of financial provision. Both of those are valid things for which to pray, but why not use the prayer of faith to enrich our spirits in love? Paul's prayer for the Philippians was that their "love may abound still more and more" (Philippians 1:9). If you ask the Father for love to abound in your heart, it will, as long as you are consistent and don't give up!

In addition to petitioning the Lord for a greater capacity to love, prayers of confession should also permeate our conversations with our Father. Confession is a word that is not extremely popular in most Christian circles, but I believe that is primarily because we have misunderstood its purpose and what it entails. We typically think of confession as simply owning up to our sins and talking about them with the Lord or with another believer, and yes, that is certainly one piece of the puzzle. But confession that occurs in the context of repentance is not something to be dreaded, or even just endured. It is actually a gift from the Lord! How wonderful God is for allowing us the opportunity to embrace forgiveness and offload the heaviness of sin by simply agreeing with His Word regarding standards of righteousness and the power of Jesus' blood! Confession is critical in the life of a believer because it builds confidence before God, which is essential if we are to feel His subtle stirrings in our spirit.

However, confession that leads to confidence before God is not limited exclusively to the grace of repentance. In fact, while repentance is the key to keeping us from getting bogged down in our sin, there is another type of confession that is meant to boost us forward into maturity. One definition of the word *confess* is simply "to proclaim." When we confess, or proclaim, the promises of God over our own lives, it awakens and calls forth a transformative faith in our spirit. Agreeing with and verbalizing God's declarations regarding who we truly are and how He views us eventually unlocks our ability to believe what He has said, resulting in a healthy, God-fearing confidence. This type of confession might look something like this: "Jesus, I am Your beloved, Your favorite one. I am the disciple whom You love. Your delight is in me. You feel the same way about me that the Father feels about You. I belong to You, and You have given Yourself to me. I am loved by You, and I am a lover of You, therefore I am successful." If you think this sounds haughty or arrogant, I would challenge you to consider the words of John the apostle. In his Gospel, John writes, "Therefore that disciple whom Jesus loved said to Peter, 'It is the Lord!'" (John 21:7). Any guess who spoke those words to Peter? It was John himself! John knew He was loved by Jesus, and he fully embraced it. So did King David. In Psalm 18:19 David writes, "He delivered me because He delighted in me."

I'll be honest. This type of confession may be difficult for a while. In fact, it may even hurt a bit until your mind is renewed and any religious spirit is driven out. I remember attending the Onething Conference at the International

House of Prayer in Kansas City in 2009, and during one of
the worship times, Cory Asbury led us in singing his song,
"Where I Belong." The bridge of the song includes the lyrics,
"I am my Beloved's and He is mine, so come into Your garden
and take delight in me."[13] As I sang the words, something in me
felt repulsed. I felt like an incredible hypocrite for suggesting
that there was anything in me that would cause God to take
delight. In all honesty, given where I was personally at that
time, there probably wasn't much. But God sees the beginning
from the end, and He fully trusts in His ability to complete
the work He has started in me. He looks at my life and sees
where I will be and not just where
I am today. As a result, He actually
enjoys me *today*, in the midst of my
weakness. I am still challenged to
believe this on a daily basis, but years
of hearing myself say and sing it has
gone a really long way. At least now I
don't feel like regurgitating. And about half the time, I believe
He actually likes me.

HE ACTUALLY
ENJOYS ME *TODAY*,
IN THE MIDST OF
MY WEAKNESS.

Finally, the Scriptures are clear that as we watch and wait
for Jesus to return, we are not to do so in isolation from other
believers. While time alone with Jesus is obviously an integral part of growing in love for Him, there is also great value
in "doing life" together with other believers. If for no other
reason, it is pretty difficult to learn to walk out the second
great commandment, to "love others as yourself," if you never
spend time with others. However, there is so much more to
why the author of Hebrews commands us to "consider how
we may spur one another on toward love and good deeds, not

---

[13] Cory Asbury, "Where I Belong," recorded 2009, track 14 on *Let Me See Your
Eyes*, Forerunner Music, compact disc.

giving up meeting together, as some are in the habit of doing, but encouraging one another—and all the more as you see the Day approaching" (Hebrews 10:24-25, NIV).

God's love is only seen in fullness when the whole body of Christ functions together. Part of our revelation of God's character and heart comes directly from the Holy Spirit, but we also get a significant portion of it from the lips of other believers, and even from our own lips as we enjoy fellowship with like-minded followers of Jesus. But our fellowship must have focus. Two dull spirits simply "hanging out" together does not equal biblical fellowship. Our fellowship must occur in the light. This does not mean that we must be fully mature before we can enjoy fellowship according to God's definition, but it does mean that we must be sincere about being wholehearted and building one another up.

Like the five wise virgins in Jesus' parable, we want to be sure that there is oil in our lamps and that we have not allowed our hearts to become distracted when He returns. My hope is that our discussion in this chapter has left you with some very practical ways to cultivate a fiery spirit and keep the oil flowing. The end goal is to sustain a fresh walk with Jesus for decades. Like David, our heart's cry should be that we are able to behold the beauty of the Lord all the days of our lives (Psalm 27:4). However, we have an enemy who seeks to derail us in our relentless pursuit of our Bridegroom. And make no mistake, he is sneaky. Paul said of him, "I am afraid, lest as the serpent [Satan] deceived Eve by his craftiness, your minds should be led astray from the simplicity and purity of devotion to Christ" (2 Corinthians 11:3, NASB). Actually, according to that verse, we really have two enemies that we must watch. Not only does Satan work to draw us off course, our natural, fleshly inclinations are to look for every opportunity to deviate from the plan. So, before we leave this chapter, I want to quickly touch on some of the common reasons why I believe many sincere believers get derailed in their pursuit of the first commandment.

Maybe we start strong and begin to notice some real growth taking place, but then something happens. We mess up. While God is not the least bit surprised, our natural bent when we know we have fallen short is to wallow in condemnation, while God simply asks us to repent, speak truth, and keep moving forward with Him. Paul tells us we have all sinned and fallen short, but the good news is that we "all are justified freely by his grace through the redemption that came by Christ Jesus" (Romans 3:24, NIV). Choosing condemnation over grace stalls our forward progression. Not only that, it allows the lies of the enemy to bear more fruit in our lives than the grace and mercy that comes through Calvary. Get up! Keep moving!

ANOTHER REASON MANY OF US GET SIDE-TRACKED AND THROWN OFF COURSE IS WE ARE NOT CAREFUL ABOUT HOW WE MANAGE OUR TIME. OURS IS A CUL-TURE THAT IS RULED BY ENTERTAINMENT.

Another reason many of us get sidetracked and thrown off course is we are not careful about how we manage our time. Ours is a culture that is ruled by entertainment. Television, movies, video games, sporting events, social media . . . the list goes on and on. None of these things is evil in and of itself, but if not kept in check, any one of them can kill our intimacy with the Lord. More than ever before, it takes focused intentionality to weed out the distractions and maintain focus on what is truly important.

If entertainment is not your poison pill, then maybe it is your job. Or your domestic responsibilities. Or your volunteer work. Or your ministry. Or sleep. Again, none of these is to be avoided completely. (I hope that is obvious.) But any one of them can be a time-sucker that leaves us with little to no time for cultivating passion for Jesus in the secret place. It is very easy to come up with justification for allowing distractions to unseat the first commandment from first place in our lives, especially when we expect it will only be momentary. However,

DON'T DISCOUNT OR DESPISE EVEN THE SMALLEST MOVEMENTS OF YOUR HEART TOWARD GOD.

more times than not, a day turns into a week, a week turns into a month, and before we know it our hearts have grown cold. As we discussed previously, you will not naturally grow in love. Unfortunately, our natural inclination is to grow cold, and we must guard our time in such a way that we battle that tendency rather than fall victim to it.

While there are certainly numerous other factors that might draw us off course once we make the decision to make loving Jesus our first priority, there is one more I would like to address before moving on: unrealistic expectations. God's process for growing our capacity to love takes time. One of the by-products of a culture that is driven by entertainment and business is that we have lost our ability to wait. Patience is sorely lacking. Therefore, when God's process takes longer than we expected, we begin to despise the process due to our exaggerated ideals regarding how quickly we "should be" maturing. While it may be easier said than done, here is my encouragement if you struggle in this regard: don't discount or despise even the smallest movements of your heart toward God. Even the most subtle stirring of our heart and the weakest "yes" to God in our spirit are supernatural events, proof that God is working in us to complete the work He began. His grace is released in our weak efforts to cooperate, and that grace will inevitably mature us at exactly the right pace if we stay the course and don't give up!

Chapter Nine

AND THE SECOND IS LIKE IT

"People are unreasonable, illogical
and self-centered. Love them anyway."

– Kent M. Keith, *The Paradoxical Commandments:
Finding Personal Meaning in a Crazy World*[14]

"I love mankind. It's people I can't stand!"

– Linus van Pelt in Charles Schultz's
The Complete Peanuts, Vol. 5: 1959-1960[15]

As we examined in a previous chapter, when Jesus is asked
the question about the greatest commandment in the Law,
He answers by quoting Deuteronomy 6:5: "You shall love the

---

[14] Kent M. Keith, *The Paradoxical Commandments: Finding Personal Meaning in a Crazy World* (Maui: Inner Ocean Publishing, 2001), 15.
[15] Charles M. Schultz, *The Complete Peanuts, Vol. 5: 1959-1960* (Seattle: Fantagraphics Books, 2006).

Lord your God with all your heart, with all your soul, and with all your strength." This would have been no surprise to His listeners, since every Jewish man, woman, and child knew that loving God and putting Him first was the primary commandment. They would have expected this answer and even agreed with it. However, what Jesus says next would have been completely unexpected: "And the second is like it: 'You shall love your neighbor as yourself.'" He essentially takes an obscure Levitical commandment (Leviticus 19:18) that had obviously been overlooked by many of His listeners and places it second only to loving God.

What's more, Jesus tells His listeners that this new commandment is "like" the first. It is second, but it is inherently linked with loving God. In fact, this commandment is so important to Jesus that He demonstrates it throughout His entire life and ministry. When He is only a very short time away from His agonizing trip to Golgotha, Jesus provides the ultimate demonstration by calling His disciples together and humbly washing their feet. After He has completed this most unselfish act, He reiterates His Matthew 22 teaching, saying, "A new commandment I give to you, that you love one another; as I have loved you, that you also love one another" (John 13:34). Jesus knew that His time with His disciples was nearing the end, and He wanted to leave no doubt in their minds how they should live out the rest of their time on earth—loving God and loving one another.

Up to this point we have focused our attention almost entirely on Jesus' first commandment, and the reason is because it is just that: first. It must be in place before anything else matters. However, with our hearts set on growing in love for God, we cannot help but grow in love for others. In fact, those who truly love Jesus will naturally love other people far more. The two commandments are inseparable, which is why Jesus discusses both when asked about the greatest commandment in the Law. You cannot emphasize one while neglecting the other. The first is always first. The second can't be first. But it also can't be tenth. *It is second.* The first cannot stand alone; it is impossible to love God and not love what He loves. It is a natural progression, as we discussed in an earlier chapter. The second also cannot stand alone, or else it will prove empty and unsustainable, leading to frustration, bitterness, and burnout. To focus solely on the second commandment, or even to let it become first in our lives, is to make our ministry an idol in our heart. God will have no others before Him, no matter how good our intentions might be. Conversely, to those who set their hearts to go after both commandments in the order in which they are intended, the Holy Spirit provides the anointing to walk them out in perfect harmony, which brings great delight to the Father and to our own hearts.

THE SECOND COMMANDMENT CANNOT STAND ALONE, OR ELSE IT WILL PROVE EMPTY AND UNSUSTAINABLE, LEADING TO FRUSTRATION, BITTERNESS, AND BURNOUT.

The Second Demonstrates the First

Before we proceed in our discussion of Jesus' second commandment, let's take a moment to quickly review the four stages in the progression of passionate love that we discussed in Chapter 3. For us to build a house that will stand, the blueprint of a heart that is fully alive in love must begin with a foundation of receiving revelation of God's love for people. Knowing how our Father thinks and feels about us is the single truth that equips our hearts to be open to the next stage in the journey, which is allowing God to impart love for Jesus to our hearts—the same love the Father has for His Son! This is the type of love that is unmoved by circumstances, persecution, or any other outward force. It results in an affection-based obedience and devotion to our Beloved, a passionate love that goes far beyond following Jesus out of a sense of duty or fear. Instead, we become free to relate to Him as a bride who is captivated by her Bridegroom, calling Him "my Husband" rather than "my Master" (Hosea 2:16).

Once we have laid the foundation of active communion between our hearts and that of our Father, we are empowered to express a meaningful, truth-based love for people as well. This love is simply a natural overflow of our hearts that comes from the joy and satisfaction we experience from loving, and being loved by, our Father in Heaven. First, we are free to love ourselves in the grace of God, understanding our inherent worth and value as beloved ones of the King. We are able to see ourselves rightly and simply agree with God's assessment of who we are. It is critical that we not resist this righteous love of self, because to do so will eventually cause our hearts to become cold. We will begin to see cracks in our foundation. After all, if we can't allow ourselves to believe that we are lovable, then how can we hold on to the reality that God is ravished by desire for us, especially when we are at our weakest? Resisting God's impartation to our hearts of love for self has the potential to spark a destructive cycle in which we begin to doubt both God's love for us and the legitimacy of our love for Him, causing us to despise ourselves even more. At a minimum, we are hindered from walking in fullness of purpose and destiny. Moreover, since we are called by Jesus to love our neighbor as we love ourselves, we also do a great disservice to both the church and the world around us when we refuse to love ourselves in a godly way.

That brings us to the focal point of this chapter: walking in love for others, confident we are loved by God, secure in the reality that our love for Him is legitimate, and free from the bondages of envy, comparison, and self-condemnation.

Overcoming the inherent selfishness of the human heart to form a heart that is marked by love for others is one of the greatest works of the Holy Spirit, and it is the ultimate proof of His activity within those who seek to follow Jesus. As we love God and ourselves, we naturally overflow in love for others. In fact, this is the only visible measurement of our invisible love for God. It is difficult to recognize and evaluate the inner workings of the heart, such as love for God and self, but since love for others can be demonstrated only through action, it is easy to see.

Loving others, which is stage four in our progression toward holy passion, is effectively a summation of the other three, and when we express that love in a manner that honors God, He takes it personally. Not only that, but it also gives us confidence before God that our love for Him is real. The Apostle John tells us in 1 John 3:18-19, "[L]et us not love in word or in tongue, but in deed and in truth. And by this we know that we are of the truth, and shall assure our hearts before Him." In other words, if you want to know the extent to which your heart is growing in love for God, consider how your actions reflect love for those around you.

Before we move on, there is one other critical dimension to loving others that we must consider: it validates our internal love for Jesus in the eyes of those around us. In other words, living a life of love for others brings some substance to our claims in the eyes of onlookers. Not to mention, it makes following Jesus seem significantly more appealing to those who might be seeking after truth.

I believe wholeheartedly that people are looking for something legitimate and meaningful to which they can give their lives in full abandonment. Of course, you and I both know that there is nothing more worthy of passionate commitment and pursuit than Jesus! But, regrettably, our claims of Jesus' worthiness to be loved and worshiped are too often coupled with indifference toward the injustice, hardship, and discouragement that surrounds us. In fact, in many cases we have difficulty expressing humility, servanthood, and authentic love to those who are members of the same family, the redeemed children of God! To quote the Apostle James (although somewhat out of context), "My Christian brothers, this is not right!" (James 3:10, NLT).

According to Jesus, the way that others will know that we are His disciples is when we love one another: "A new commandment I give you, that you love one another . . . By this all will know that you are My disciples" (John 13:34-35). Certainly, there are "good people" in the world who have not made the decision to follow Jesus, so it is quite possible that people will not necessarily make the connection between our love for others and our commitment to Jesus. However, one thing is guaranteed: people will certainly know we are *not* His followers when we regularly treat others with contempt, or even with indifference. Or, worse yet, they might accept our claims that we follow Jesus and assume that our character and actions accurately reflect His. Because Jesus loves people so passionately and certainly doesn't want those who bear His name dissuading others from knowing Him, this is serious business. We might stumble from time to time when it comes to loving others, especially the more "difficult" folks, but if we are consistently having difficulty in this area, it is almost certainly an indicator of a disconnect between our hearts and our Father's, and it demands swift attention and repentance.

It Takes God

Loving others well is a lifestyle that must flow from a dynamic, persistent relationship with the Holy Spirit. It is not a sporadic disposition or an event that we periodically gear up for, but a day in, day out way of life. While the occasional mission trip or outreach is certainly a great way to communicate and display the love of God to a particular group of people, God has set the bar much higher. It is relatively easy to love people for a few hours at a time, especially when we will likely never see them again or enter into the messiness that actual relationships bring. But what about those we "do life" with daily? This is the arena in which true love for Jesus and for those He loves is best displayed.

Our human nature is to take for granted and, at times, even despise those with whom we spend time on a regular basis. There is nothing in us, apart from the work of the Holy Spirit in our hearts, that causes us to naturally exhibit humility and a servant's heart toward those whom we know and who know us best. While it seems counterintuitive that we would find it easier to love someone we barely know than someone we care for deeply, the truth is that while our closest relationships have the most potential to bring great joy, they also bring the most frustration, heartache, and inconvenience. We typically have little difficulty loving the man on the street or the child in the soup kitchen line, but things get a little sticky when we have to show love to our spouse who just asked us to empty the dishwasher when the game is on television. Still, in typical fashion, Jesus calls us to consistency in love, even in the most trying of circumstances.

Based on years of conversations and personal relationships, I believe that consistently loving those we care for most is a universal struggle. At the same time, I am fully aware that there are some who may read this and not be able to relate. Maybe you are excellent when it comes to steadily loving those in your home and in your tightest circles (although I would be interested to know if your closest friends and family members would agree). If that is the case, bravo! I have much to learn from you. However, since you are human, I am guessing there is at least one individual out there with whom you have your struggles.

The difficult coworker who is quick to take credit while lacking in actual contribution.

The church member who pats you on the back when you walk in the door, but stabs you in it behind closed doors.

The guy who cut you off in traffic or stole "your" space in the crowded parking lot.

The lady behind the counter at the fast food joint who had a bad attitude, then made matters even worse by messing up your order.

The telemarketer who continues to try to make the sale, even after you have politely indicated your disinterest several times during the brief conversation.

The bottom line? Consistent love for others is difficult apart from God. Scratch that. It is *impossible*. In a previous chapter we discussed that it takes the supernatural intervention of the Holy Spirit on the human heart to empower us to love God. Since God is consistent in His love for and goodness toward us, and we struggle to love Him apart from Him, shouldn't we conclude that it certainly takes God to love imperfect and unsteady humans, especially if we are to love them in the way God defines? Nowhere does God indicate a requirement that we consistently enjoy the people around us, but He does call us to consistent love. Walking this out requires the Spirit's power to energize us.

CONSISTENT LOVE FOR OTHERS IS DIFFICULT APART FROM GOD. SCRATCH THAT. IT IS *IMPOSSIBLE*.

Next to John 3:16, I think Matthew 7:12 might be the most well-known Scripture in the Bible. In fact, it may actually be the most well-known, as it is often referenced by believers and nonbelievers alike. It is so often referenced that we have even given it a name: the "Golden Rule." It is a wonderful Scripture with so much relevance, not only at the time it was spoken, but also today. However, like many Scriptures, this one loses a great deal of its power if it is not considered in the context in which it was given. Jesus speaks these famous words as part of His Sermon on the Mount, in which he calls His followers to an all-consuming relationship with God:

> Ask, and it will be given to you; seek, and you will find; knock, and it will be opened to you. For everyone who asks receives, and he who seeks finds, and to him who knocks it will be opened. Or what man is there among you who, if his son asks for bread, will give him a stone? Or if he asks for a fish, will he give him a serpent? If you then, being evil, know how to give good gifts to your children, how much more will your Father who is in heaven give good things to those who ask Him! Therefore, whatever you want men to do to you, do also to them, for this is the Law and the Prophets (Matthew 7:7-12).

As you can see, in this passage Jesus begins by teaching us that the Father gives good things to those who petition Him in prayer. He then transitions into the "Golden Rule" through the use of the word "therefore," indicating that what He is about to say is directly tied to what He has just finished saying. Given this transition, we can clearly see that the call to walk in love and "do unto others" is given in the context of a call to prayer. The foundation of the commandment is once again tied to a revelation of the Father's love and His supernatural provision that comes through a prayer life based on trusting His leadership in our lives.

We are created to be responders. God initiates. We respond. It is true from the very beginning. God breathes life, and our heart starts beating. God draws our hearts to Jesus, and we follow. Sure, we initiate from time to time, but my experience has proven that those things which are pursued for any reason other than as a response to God are almost always unfulfilling, and typically unsuccessful. This dynamic certainly holds true in to our attempts at loving others well. We need our emotions to be stirred and strengthened regularly by the subtle impressions of the Holy Spirit.

As Paul states in Romans 5:5, "The love of God has been poured out in our hearts by the Holy Spirit who was given to us." This is a constant pouring out that occurs only in the context of relationship. First and foremost, Jesus calls us to an ongoing encounter of love with a Person—Himself. As we experience that encounter, we are naturally motivated by the gratitude and joy of being loved by God to love Him in return, and as that relationship is strengthened, we are energized to sustain compassionate love for those around us. It takes God to love God, and it takes God to love others. You may be able to "be nice" without supernatural activity (although that alone is difficult for many of us), but while it is certainly good to be nice, it is not enough. It is very possible that you might *mean* well apart from a dynamic relationship with the Holy Spirit, but you will never *love* well.

Loving others well requires that we undergo a comprehensive reordering of how we think and process life. This requires dogged intentionality. By nature, humans are quite self-absorbed (often while actually despising ourselves), and we require the power of the Holy Spirit to walk out a selfless life of love. Loving well means that we value the longings of others for significance, acceptance, and success as being every bit as important as our own. This does not come naturally or easily. However, as we consistently reach to love others, we are naturally freed from the prison of self-consumption, and, in time, we even learn to enjoy living with an "others first" mentality and approach to life.

Jesus' radical command to love other people as we love ourselves touches at the core of our being and exposes a deep root system of sin in our hearts. Seeking to follow that command quickly reveals our weakness and spiritual lack. While our initial response may be to say, "No thanks!" and wonder why Jesus would be so harsh as to ask us to do something we are incapable of, the reality is that this is one of the kindest things He could do. Being confronted with our weakness creates deep humility and helps us see our great need more clearly. It allows us to experience God's tenderness and compassion as He loves us in the midst of our weakness, which creates gratitude in our hearts that opens a door to encounter God in a way that the ungrateful heart cannot. In Matthew 5:3, Jesus tells His followers that those who are "poor in spirit" will actually inherit the kingdom of Heaven. So, by forcing us to wrestle with the ugliness of our hearts, Jesus empowers us to confront it, defeat it, and, in doing so, bring the kingdom to earth in a significant way.

> WHILE OUR INITIAL RESPONSE MAY BE TO SAY, "NO THANKS!" AND WONDER WHY JESUS WOULD BE SO HARSH AS TO ASK US TO DO SOMETHING WE ARE INCAPABLE OF, THE REALITY IS THAT THIS IS ONE OF THE KINDEST THINGS HE COULD DO.

Did You Learn to Love?

What is wonderful about seeking to follow Jesus' commandment to love others is that it not only brings the kingdom of Heaven to earth in a real and tangible way, but when we love according to His definition, it carries a ripple effect that extends into eternity. For this reason, when all is said and done, love is all that truly matters. The Apostle Paul makes this reality quite clear in 1 Corinthians 13, which is referred to by many as "the love chapter":

> Though I speak with the tongues of men and of angels, but have not love, I have become sounding brass or a clanging cymbal. And though I have the gift of prophecy, and understand all mysteries and all knowledge, and though I have all faith, so that I could remove mountains, but have not love, I am nothing. And though I bestow all my goods to feed the poor, and though I give my body to be burned, but have not love, it profits me nothing (1 Corinthians 13:1-3).

Prophecy. Wisdom. Knowledge. Faith. Generosity. Selflessness. All important, yet all of no profit if not accompanied by love.

Paul continues by expounding upon what real and lasting love looks like: "Love suffers long and is kind; love does not envy; love does not parade itself, is not puffed up; does not behave rudely, does not seek its own, is not provoked, thinks no evil; does not rejoice in iniquity, but rejoices in the truth; bears all things, believes all things, hopes all things, endures all things" (1 Corinthians 13:4-7). If this passage is familiar to you, please fight the temptation to blow past it without truly considering what Paul is saying. This is one of the single most precious verses in all of Scripture, for in it, Paul tells us how our lives will look if we are truly loving toward those around us. It should be a jumping-off point for hours of meaningful prayer and meditation for anyone who desires to follow in the footsteps of Jesus!

First, Paul tells us that love "suffers long." This is the passive aspect of love's character, as it entails showing mercy rather than giving others what they deserve. It speaks of perseverance and patience, bearing with others no matter how difficult it may seem. He then describes love as "kind." This is the active aspect of what it means to love: giving to others what they do not deserve. We come in contact daily with plenty of people who may not "deserve" love, but Paul (and Jesus) tells us to give it anyway. Be kind, even when the situation doesn't seem to call for kindness, because *every* encounter calls for kindness. Let's face it, there are plenty of times when we are the ones undeserving of love. It's nice when someone shows it anyway.

Then, as if he knows there will be folks like me who still don't really get it, Paul gives us specific examples of what love is—and is not. Love is not jealous. It is neither boastful nor proud. Love is not rude, and it does not demand its own way. Love is not irritable. It does not dwell on evil, and it is not excited about or indifferent toward injustice. Instead, love rejoices when truth triumphs. Love never gives up and never loses faith. Love is always hopeful and endures through every circumstance.

As we can see, Paul sets the bar a little higher than just being nice and meeting needs. Love requires more than just sentimental humanism, which lacks an emphasis on a relationship with Jesus based on God's terms. We are right to focus our energies, efforts, and resources on meeting physical needs, but woe to us if we reduce love to that aim alone. After all, even the Antichrist's system will be based on secular humanism and "compassion." According to Paul, "love rejoices when truth triumphs," and the ultimate truth is that Jesus is Lord, and He *will* have His inheritance in a people who voluntarily say yes to His sacrifice and leadership. Not to mention that people are eternal, spiritual beings who need more than just to have their physical needs met.

The kind of love that Paul advocates is used by God to awaken the human heart to the truth about Jesus. It naturally draws people to His goodness rather than to the "goodness" of man. While it is true that God created us to connect with one another, no matter what other needs we may meet, *everyone's* profound need is to connect with God. When we help others make that connection, not only are their immediate circumstances impacted, they are invited into an encounter that impacts them for eternity!

But wait . . . there's more!

After outlining in detail everything that love is and everything it is not, Paul concludes with this simple phrase: "Love never fails" (1 Corinthians 13:8). Does this imply that love is always received by others or that it is always effective in the eyes of man? Of course not. The ultimate act of love was demonstrated on a Roman cross on a Friday afternoon on a lonely hill just outside of Jerusalem, and countless numbers through the centuries have dismissed it without so much as a second thought. So what does Paul mean? Love never fails because every movement of our hearts in love is remembered and rewarded by God forever at the judgment seat of Christ, whether it is received by people in this life or not. No investment of love is forgotten, wasted, or lost in God's sight. This is precisely why Paul tells us in the passage above that if he were to operate in every spiritual gift on the list and give everything he owns to the poor, without love, it would still "profit him nothing." The only thing that "profits us" is what God sees and remembers, and what God sees and remembers is love according to His terms.

When my day comes, I am convinced Jesus will not be impressed with any abilities I may have demonstrated while on the earth, no matter how "spiritual" they may have appeared. He will not ask me how I went about improving my speaking or writing skills. He will not be concerned with any prophetic abilities I might have exhibited, how much money I gave away, or whether I served on a sufficient number of mission teams. I believe there is a single criterion by which my life and ministry will be judged, and it is my answer to this question: "Did you learn to love?" How I answer that question will summarize the entire value of my short time here on earth. If you accept that Jesus was serious when He told us that all of the Law and Prophets are summarized in His commandments to love God and love others, then I would encourage you to wrestle with your answer to that question as well. Are you learning to love?

Who Is My Neighbor?

As we wrap up our examination of Jesus' commandment to love our neighbor as ourselves, it might be helpful to close this chapter by examining the heart of what Jesus was getting at when He used the phrase "your neighbor." It is interesting to me, yet not surprising, that Jesus seems to leave this commandment somewhat open-ended. As with the many other times I read the discourses of Jesus in the Gospels, I am left somewhat frustrated. I like black and white, clear-cut direction, and Jesus is often not willing to provide it. At least not without first allowing the listener to struggle with His teachings for a bit. He provides us the opportunity to ask questions, and these questions typically reveal something about our hearts that we might not otherwise have occasion to confront.

It's kind of mean of Him, really. Yet, at the same time, it is the most gracious thing that a loving God who is concerned primarily with the state of our hearts—and only secondarily with our actions—could do.

If you aren't interested in being challenged and having to face some harsh realities about yourself, Jesus is not really your best choice of

IF YOU ARE MORE CONCERNED WITH *LOOKING* RIGHTEOUS THAN YOU ARE WITH *BEING* RIGHTEOUS, MY ADVICE WOULD BE TO AVOID JESUS LIKE THE PLAGUE.

folks to hang with. If you are more concerned with *looking* righteous than you are with *being* righteous, my advice would be to avoid Jesus like the plague. Or at least keep your mouth shut when you see Him (but that may not work either; see Matthew 9:4). If you doubt me, just ask the expert in the law who challenged Jesus in Luke 10:25-37.

> And behold, a certain lawyer stood up and tested Him, saying, "Teacher, what shall I do to inherit eternal life?"
>
> He said to him, "What is written in the law? What is your reading of it?"
>
> So he answered and said, "You shall love the Lord your God with all your heart, with all your soul, with all your strength, and with all your mind, and your neighbor as yourself."
>
> And He said to him, "You have answered rightly; do this and you will live."
>
> But he, wanting to justify himself, said to Jesus, "And who is my neighbor?"
>
> Then Jesus answered and said: "A certain man went down from Jerusalem to Jericho, and fell among thieves, who stripped him of his clothing, wounded him, and departed, leaving him half dead. Now by chance a certain priest came down that road. And when he saw him, he passed by on the other side. Likewise a Levite, when he arrived at the place, came and looked, and passed by on the other side. But a certain Samaritan, as he journeyed, came where he was. And when he saw him, he had compassion. So he went to him and bandaged his wounds, pouring on oil and wine; and he set him on his own animal, brought him to an inn, and took care of him. On the next day, when he departed, he took out two denarii, gave them to the innkeeper, and said to him, 'Take care of him; and whatever more you spend, when I come again, I will repay you.' So which of these three do you think was neighbor to him who fell among the thieves?"

> And he said, "He who showed mercy on him."
> Then Jesus said to him, "Go and do likewise."

Have you noticed that when people in the Scriptures stand up to "test" Jesus, it normally does not end well for them? They almost never get the response they were looking for. Sometimes, as in this encounter, the tester gets no response at all to the question he asked of the One being tested. Sometimes it seems as though Jesus wasn't even listening. But He was. He is. He always is. And, on the contrary, His answers typically reveal that *we* are the ones who may not have been listening.

Before we get too comfortable sitting back and chuckling at the silliness of the teacher of the law in this story, let's do some quick self-examination. Has this guy really done anything that we have not? I'm guessing none of us have ever had the audacity (or opportunity) to question Jesus face to face, but for most of us, our actions and inner struggles reveal our tendency to test Him regularly. Have you ever read a passage of Scripture that challenged you and spent hours, or even days, trying to rationalize or explain it away? I have. In fact, many of us have developed full-blown doctrines of faith around trying to explain away difficult passages of Scripture. In fact, in times past, I have even found myself engaged in an effort to persuade others to embrace my doctrines of comfortability in order to help assuage any guilt I might experience from their fervor. Perhaps Dr. Martyn Lloyd-Jones puts it best in his challenging discussion on Jesus' Sermon on the Mount: "There are ideas of Christianity far removed from the New Testament which are held by many and which cause them to persecute those who are trying in sincerity and truth to follow the Lord Jesus Christ along the narrow way."[16]

---

[16] Martyn Lloyd-Jones, *Studies in the Sermon on the Mount* (Grand Rapids: William B. Eerdmans Publishing Company, 1976), 116.

The truth is, following Jesus is difficult. If you read a passage of Scripture that challenges you, you would probably be well-advised to assume it is even more challenging than it seems at first. After all, if walking in the ways of Jesus were easy, we wouldn't need Him in the first place.

Now, with that out of the way, maybe we can identify a little more with the teacher of the law and his attempt to justify himself before Jesus.

The teacher of the law asks Jesus a simple question, and at first, he receives what seems to be a simple answer.

Teacher: "What must I do to inherit eternal life?"

Jesus: "Well, what do you think?"

Teacher: "Hmm . . . Love God and love my neighbor?"

Jesus: "Yep. Sounds good to me."

The teacher would do well to just exit the conversation at this point, but He knows there is more to the story, and he has obviously been wrestling with it. This commandment to "love thy neighbor" could range in difficulty from simple to severe, and it all depends on the definition of one small word: *neighbor*. If by "neighbor" Jesus means the people I hang out with regularly and who seem to like me and agree with me, then all is well. On the other hand, if He has the nerve to tell me I need to love the ones who don't look, act, and smell like me, then we have an issue. God forbid I have to love someone who thinks differently than I do and challenges me regularly. Surely He can't possibly mean *that*! Interestingly, it seems as though Jesus leaves the man to draw his own conclusions about what the commandment means—at least until he attempts to justify himself by asking yet another question.

Teacher: "And who is my neighbor?"

Jesus: "Funny you should ask. Let me tell you a story . . . "

What follows is the passage we looked at above, the well-known story of the Good Samaritan. Like many familiar stories in the Bible, it is relatively easy for many of us to breeze past this wonderful teaching of Jesus with a dismissive "yeah, I know that one," but let's be careful not to do that. There is much for us to learn from really digging in to this passage.

If we truly want our hearts to grow in love, it is important that we ask questions of the One who *is* love. In this regard, although his motives were not pure, the teacher of the law does well. However, as we inquire of the Lord, it is critical that we not only ask questions, but that we ask the *right* questions. Given that Jesus seems to dismiss the man's question with a story and a question of His own, I think it's safe to assume this is something the teacher in this encounter did not do. In addition, as we ask questions of the Lord, we must be willing to accept that His answer might completely change everything we have held dear. I am relatively sure the teacher of the law would back me up here.

Jesus is very intentional in the characters he chooses for His story. First, there is a man who is walking down the road from Jerusalem to Jericho. Based on his origin and destination, it is safe to assume the man is Jewish. The man falls among thieves and is beaten and left for dead. Shortly after this incident takes place, a priest passes by on the same road. It is the man's lucky day, right? Wrong. The priest, a fellow Jew, dismisses the man and continues down the road. But that's OK, because not far behind is a Levite. Yes, another Jew, and probably a pious one at that. And yet . . . another Jew who passes by and does nothing.

Remember, the question the teacher of the law asked was, "Who is my neighbor?" Jesus has just responded by telling a story in which two men whom the teacher would have admired and identified with passed by another man who was in need. My guess is the teacher probably is assuming Jesus would admire the two men in the story also. Priest. Levite. Surely these men serve as an example of holy living. If I'm the teacher, I'm starting to assume at this point that if a couple of righteous Jews did not stop to help another Jew who was in desperate need, then this whole "loving thy neighbor" thing may not be so bad after all. My thought process might go something like this: Jesus told me to love my neighbor. I asked Him whom that would include. He just told me a story about two great guys who pass by one of their own. They weren't loving toward the man, so he must not have been a neighbor. Wow. My "neighbors" must be a pretty small group.

Then, as He often does, Jesus switches gears.

After the two Jewish men pass by their fellow Jew, a Samaritan comes strolling by. This would have immediately captured the attention of Jesus' audience, because Jews and Samaritans were not exactly buddies. In fact, a fierce and long-standing hatred that dated back to the days of the patriarchs existed between them. Why would Jesus introduce this guy into the story about whom I should consider a neighbor? You are treading on thin ice here, Jesus. Be careful.

Sure enough, the Samaritan man stops when he sees the beaten Jewish man. Not only does he stop, he has compassion. Not only does he have compassion, he takes action. Significant action. He bandages the man up, takes him to the next town, and pays for any expenses incurred while the man recovers. In short, he loves well.

Teacher: "OK, Jesus. We get it. You are doing that whole 'love your enemy' thing again, huh? Well, we weren't really big fans of that whole message before, but now you are going off the deep end. In case you forgot, the question posed was in regard to whom we should consider our neighbor, and here you are talking about Samaritans. Speaking of Samaritans, what's with you making the Samaritan the hero of the story? That probably isn't going to go very far in helping you grow your ministry here in Jerusalem. Now, would you please just answer the question?"

Jesus: "Nope. But I have one for you. Which of the three men who passed by the beaten man was a neighbor to him?"

Teacher: "Ugh! I hate it when you do this! The answer is obvious, right? It's the one who showed the man mercy."

Jesus: "Yep. What's also obvious is that you need a heart adjustment. Quit asking questions aimed at letting yourself off the hook, and get to doing what matters!"

OK, maybe that's not *exactly* how it went, but you get the picture.

Jesus does not want us to be concerned about nailing down the definition of whom we are to consider our neighbor before we decide to live a life of love toward others. In fact, it would be impossible to do so, because it seems to me from this story that our neighbor is anyone with whom we come in contact. So the question we must ask as we seek to walk in love for others is not to whom we should be a neighbor, but how we might be a better neighbor to everyone we meet.

THE QUESTION WE MUST ASK AS WE SEEK TO WALK IN LOVE FOR OTHERS IS NOT TO WHOM WE SHOULD BE A NEIGHBOR, BUT HOW WE MIGHT BE A BETTER NEIGHBOR TO EVERYONE WE MEET.

The group of people collectively known as our "neighbors" is a significantly bigger circle than we might think, and it is not at all unlike God to direct our paths in such a way that they intersect with those completely unlike us. Or, worse yet, someone completely contrary to who we are and what we believe. In fact, I think He kind of enjoys it. As we grow in experiential knowledge of His love for us and allow it to spill out of us onto others, I think we will naturally learn to enjoy it as well!

Chapter Ten

IT'S ABOUT THE ENCOUNTER

"There is an essential connection between experiencing God, loving God, and trusting God. You will trust God only as much as you love him. And you will love him to the extent you have touched him, rather that he has touched you."

– Brennan Manning, *The Ragamuffin Gospel: Good News for the Bedraggled, Beat-Up, and Burnt Out*[17]

I am confident that by this point you are a firm believer in the reality that all love flows from the Father, and it is His love alone that unlocks our hearts to love Him in return. I am sure that the importance of loving God on His terms is quite evident. I assume you are convinced of the benefits we receive when we embrace the fasted lifestyle and choose growing in love over relaxing in compromise and complacency. My sincere hope is that you have read something that compels you

---

[17] Brennan Manning, *The Ragamuffin Gospel: Good News for the Bedraggled, Beat-Up, and Burnt Out* (Colorado Springs: Multnomah Books, 1990), 105.

to make any necessary adjustments to begin to truly love God with all of your heart, soul, mind, and strength, knowing that God is the source of all the grace and supernatural empowering you need. In short, my desire in sharing these pages is that the Holy Spirit has used them to fan the flame of passion for Jesus in your heart. If that is indeed the case, then I am tempted to ask you to throw this book aside and go drink deeply from the wellspring of His Word, enjoying His presence and allowing Him to enjoy yours! However, in the hope that the Holy Spirit can use just a few more thoughts to pour fuel on the fire, I offer the following.

In Mark 10:46-52, we read about Jesus' encounter with a blind man named Bartimaeus:

> Now they came to Jericho. As He went out of Jericho with His disciples and a great multitude, blind Bartimaeus, the son of Timaeus, sat by the road begging. And when he heard that it was Jesus of Nazareth, he began to cry out and say, "Jesus, Son of David, have mercy on me!"
>
> Then many warned him to be quiet; but he cried out all the more, "Son of David, have mercy on me!"
>
> So Jesus stood still and commanded him to be called.
>
> Then they called the blind man, saying to him, "Be of good cheer. Rise, He is calling you."
>
> And throwing aside his garment, he rose and came to Jesus.
>
> So Jesus answered and said to him, "What do you want Me to do for you?"
>
> The blind man said to Him, "Rabboni, that I may receive my sight."
>
> Then Jesus said to him, "Go your way; your faith has made you well." And immediately he received his sight and followed Jesus on the road.

As I have been working on this book, I have naturally been reading all of Scripture through the lens of the Great

Commandment, asking the Holy Spirit to help me grow in love for Jesus in each of the areas I have described. As a result, I noticed something in Jesus' encounter with Bartimaeus that I had not seen before. For years I have read this passage and heard it preached as evidence of the importance and power of faith in the life of the believer. Obviously, this is an undeniable reality that is found here. After all, Jesus Himself tells Bartimaeus that his faith is what made him well. In fact, the message seems so simple that it is easy to just move on and pat Bartimaeus on the back for having great faith. We love stories like this one, especially in our Western culture, don't we? We are inspired by ordinary people in the Scriptures who have such great faith that God seemingly has little choice but to respond favorably to their request. In fact, we have built doctrines and denominations around stories like this one. If we just have enough faith, God will heal us or our loved ones. Right? Furthermore, if He doesn't come through, well, we obviously did not have enough faith. Because faith heals. No healing equals no faith.

Tell that to the parents who have prayed for years for their little girl to be healed of leukemia, taken communion with her countless times, called the elders to lay hands on her and pray, lost endless hours of sleep crying out to the Lord for her healing . . . only to gather around her graveside with incomprehensible grief in their hearts. What's that? You wouldn't say such a thing to them? Yeah, me neither.

When I first came to know Jesus, I was immediately submerged deep into what was being referred to by many as the "faith movement." The teaching I heard was so wonderful! As a new follower of Jesus who had no grounding whatsoever in the Scriptures, I came to believe that I could pretty well just ask God for whatever I wanted, and as long as I "had faith," He had pretty well obligated Himself to fulfill my every wish. I came to idolize the "successful" preachers who had the

Armani suits and Rolex watches, who flew to their next meetings in private jets, and who seemed to have direct lines to the throne room. I longed to be like them, focusing all of my attention and energy on becoming a man of great faith. If only I could grow my faith to the same level as theirs, then I could do great things for God! I could literally change the world!

Then came the time when what I believed almost caused me to walk away from what I believed.

If you embrace the idea that your faith can positively impact the world and then consistently see things change for the better when you pray, then that would be a pretty awesome experience, right? Well, what if you pray with every bit of faith you can muster and nothing happens? Yep, pretty discouraging. Especially if you have been told that when God doesn't move, it is due to a lack of faith. And especially when your prayers are in regard to an issue that hits close to home.

You see, my name is Kyle, and my mother was an alcoholic.

Lest you be left with the impression that she was some sort of deadbeat, or even anything short of amazing, let me clarify. My mother is one of my heroes. For reasons that are still somewhat unclear to me (and that I don't much care about anymore), things did not work out between her and my father (also a great individual), leaving her with the daunting responsibility of raising a child as a single mother. While she had the help of two of the greatest grandparents ever conceived in the mind of the Creator, it was still a significant challenge, and she faced it with tenacity and determination. In a time when it was extremely rare for a woman to scale the corporate ladder in a significant way, she became a vice president at one of the major banks in our city. In my mind, the way she managed to balance the demands of the workplace with her responsibilities as a single parent was nothing short of fascinating. She provided for my every need. She made great sacrifices for me. She encouraged me. She loved me well. I am forever grateful, and I miss her terribly.

I'm not sure if it happened gradually, or if one day something just snapped. Whatever the case, addiction reared its ugly head, and one of the greats was slowly taken down. I don't think the details of that process deserve mention here, so suffice it to say that I prayed earnestly (although sporadically, I admit) for her for more than seventeen years. I asked the Lord to heal her and set her free from her addiction time and time again. It didn't happen. And in 2010, just a few months after my grandmother passed away from Alzheimer's, I held the frail, delicate hand of the woman who, for so many years, had symbolized the very essence of strength and resilience, as she lay dying in a dimly lit hospital room. I cried out to the Lord to heal her. I reasoned with Him, making sure He understood how much glory He could receive by having her get up and walk out the front door. I commanded her liver to regenerate and for all of her normal bodily functions to come into alignment with God's design. I cried. I reasoned. I commanded. She died.

> I COMMANDED HER LIVER TO REGENERATE AND FOR ALL OF HER NORMAL BODILY FUNCTIONS TO COME INTO ALIGNMENT WITH GOD'S DESIGN. I CRIED. I REASONED. I COMMANDED. SHE DIED.

To say I was devastated by the events of 2010 would certainly be an understatement. In a few short months, I lost the two people I most admired and looked to for support for the majority of my life. My heart was broken. My compass suddenly felt uncalibrated. The story did not end the way it was supposed to. While I know my faith wavered from time to time, it had mostly been consistent and strong. I truly believed that God could heal my mother. I even believed He *would*. He did it for Bartimaeus. Why not for me?

One of the primary foundations of the kingdom of God is that Jesus' leadership is good, that His sovereign actions are always motivated by perfect love and infallible wisdom. However, when your world is shaken the way mine was (and we all experience shaking), it is easy to become offended at that leadership. When God doesn't act the way we think He ought to act, our minds are naturally faced with a dilemma.

Just ask the disciples of John the Baptist.

When their beloved John is in prison and receives reports of the miracles Jesus is performing, he sends his disciples to ask Jesus, "Are You the Coming One, or do we look for another?" (Matthew 11:3). Why do they ask such a question? Maybe John's faith was wavering a bit. Or maybe John was not wavering at all, but wanted to help his disciples learn for themselves the truth about who Jesus really is. While my personal belief is that the latter is true, I'm not sure how much it really matters. Either way, the question was asked, and Jesus answers by rattling off several points about His ministry and how He is fulfilling the words of the prophet Isaiah. He wraps up with these words: "And blessed is he who is not offended because of Me" (Matthew 11:6).

JESUS KNOWS THERE IS A TIME COMING IN WHICH THE MEN TO WHOM HE SPEAKS WILL NEED TO HOLD ON TO THE WORDS HE HAS SPOKEN. HE KNOWS HE WILL NOT BE INTERVENING ON JOHN'S BEHALF. JOHN IS GOING TO DIE.

Why would Jesus make such a statement to John's disciples? He has just told them how He has given sight to the blind, made the lame able to walk, cleansed the lepers, and raised the dead. Other than the Pharisees, who could possibly be offended by that? But Jesus knows there is a time coming in which the men to whom

He speaks will need to hold on to the words He has spoken. He knows He will not be intervening on John's behalf. John is going to die. Jesus could have done something to stop it, but He chooses not to, and John's disciples will have to struggle through the offense they experience as a result. Since offense makes us unable to experience gratitude, and since we can't possibly grow in love without a grateful heart, Jesus knows that how John's disciples respond to these events will affect their lives deeply from that point forward.

Why does Jesus come through for someone like Bartimaeus while leaving His friend, John, to die in prison? More importantly to me, why does He heal Bartimaeus and seemingly ignore my prayers for Him to heal my mother and grandmother? At the time of this writing, it has been about seven years since the dreadful months in which my world fell apart around me, and over the years I have considered that question a great deal. Do you want to know the conclusion I have come to?

I don't know.

That's right. I have no idea why God didn't come through the way I wanted Him to. And I have struggled with it. A lot. But, as I have struggled, God has begun to teach me a couple of invaluable lessons. First, Jesus allows our minds to be offended in order to reveal our hearts. He acts in certain ways and allows certain things in our lives in order to cause our hunger to grow and to force our unperceived offenses with Him to the surface so that they can be dealt with. How we respond determines whether we are delivered from those offenses or they consume us. Also, while Jesus did commend Bartimaeus for his great faith, elsewhere He taught His disciples that even faith the size of a mustard seed can move mountains. I'm not a horticulturist, but I know that a mustard seed is pretty small, which leads me to believe that it is ultimately not the *amount* of faith we can muster that matters, but truly knowing the *Object* of it. I know a number of preachers who would cry "Blasphemy!" at that assertion, but it is a conclusion with which I have become quite comfortable and confident.

Please understand what I am trying to communicate here. By no means am I attempting to minimize the importance of faith in the life of a believer. We are saved by grace, through faith. Without faith, we cannot please God (Hebrews 11:6) and we cannot experience grace. However, it is grace that ultimately saves us, not faith. Faith just leads us to grace. Or better yet, it leads us to the Source of all grace. In short, faith leads us to *encounter*.

Think about this for a moment: did Bartimaeus have faith before he met Jesus in the city of Jericho and was healed? Of course he did. If he did not, why would he have sought Jesus in the first place? Nevertheless, until he encountered Jesus, he remained blind. For Bartimaeus, faith ultimately led to an encounter with Jesus, and the end result was healing in his body. In my case, desperation, combined with at least a mustard seed-sized amount of faith, led to encounter as well. While my mother was not set free from the addiction that eventually took her life (at least not on this side of eternity), encountering Jesus gave me the strength that was necessary to navigate the darkest year of my life. Do I still wish God would have healed her? Of course! However, I am grateful beyond words for the emotional healing that has taken place in my heart over the past seven years by honestly struggling through such a painful loss with the Holy Spirit as my Comforter. Without the loss I experienced, I would not have had the opportunity to learn about the Father's great love for me in the way I have. Moreover, experiencing His love in the midst of tragedy has caused me to love Him even deeper than before. I still am not completely clear why Bartimaeus was granted his request while I was not, but I am clear about this one thing—it is not about the miracle or the answered prayer. It is about the encounter.

My greatest fear in writing a book like this is that the reader might be tempted to reduce the contents presented to some sort of formula or checklist. To be sure, there are principles and promises presented in the Word of God which we must seek to understand and embrace. It is important to study and know the Word. It is critical that we do what it says. When we do, the results that God outlines will surely follow. We can and should expect that the Lord will do what He says He will do. But God help us if we reduce following Jesus to an "I do this, and God will do that" relationship. That is a miserable way to live, and it is immeasurably far from God's intention for our lives. Please don't do it.

> GOD HELP US IF WE REDUCE FOLLOWING JESUS TO AN "I DO THIS, AND GOD WILL DO THAT" RELATIONSHIP. THAT IS A MISERABLE WAY TO LIVE, AND IT IS IMMEASURABLY FAR FROM GOD'S INTENTION FOR OUR LIVES.

For the follower of Jesus, all of life is about regularly encountering Him. We position ourselves for encounter by resting in God's love for us, learning to love Him on His terms, pouring out love on those around us—all the things we have discussed in this book. But please, whatever you do, don't reduce the principles in this book to a formula or checklist. Instead, embrace them as a pathway to encounter.

Thanks for coming along on this journey. My prayer for you as we part ways here is that your mind will in no way be "led astray from the simplicity and purity of devotion to Christ" (2 Corinthians 11:3, NASB). In other words, I pray that nothing will be able to distract you from keeping the main thing the main thing. The main thing is not healing. The main thing is not fasting. The main thing is not prophecy. It is not good works. It's not success in ministry. It's not great knowledge of the Scriptures. It's not even seeking after "great faith."

All of these are wonderful, and each should be a normal part of the life of a Jesus follower. Nevertheless, if you set your heart on any of them, you are likely to be disappointed. Even devastated. Love, on the other hand, will never disappoint, because love never fails. Love alone is the lover's reward, and consistent encounters with the Lover of our souls are our highest aim. The Scriptures command us to "forget not all His benefits" (Psalm 103:2), and there are many. But no benefit can surpass being rooted and established in love, knowing that you are loved by God and a true lover of God. Do whatever it takes to have *that*. So, if the principles in this book have been helpful to you, then you are welcome. If not, my apologies. Either way, the path you take from here is yours to choose. I pray it leads you into deeper encounter with the inexhaustible love of the Bridegroom God who is ravished with desire for you!

About Kyle McNutt

Kyle McNutt has been involved in ministry for more than twenty years. He is the founder and Executive Director of encounterGOD, a ministry devoted to helping Christ followers develop a deeper level of intimacy with Jesus.

Kyle began his ministry as a volunteer in youth ministry at Trinity Church in Lubbock, Texas in the fall of 1994. Through his seven years at Trinity, he served as an intern in both youth and children's ministry while also attending Texas Tech University. During his senior year at Tech, Kyle became the director of Frontline Ministries, one of the primary outreach and evangelism ministries at Trinity. As director of Frontline, Kyle oversaw various efforts, including the weekly Adopt-a-Block outreach, Sidewalk Sunday School, and the daily after-school program for at-risk neighborhood children.

Shortly before graduating from Texas Tech in May 1999 with a B.B.A. in Management Information Systems, Kyle met Carey Taylor, and upon marrying in May 2000, Kyle and Carey left Trinity to join Live Oak Community Church in Lubbock. Both Kyle and Carey spent several years as volunteers in the student ministry of Live Oak, and Kyle eventually took over the role of Director of Student Ministries in July 2003. In March 2004, the elders of Live Oak felt led to license and ordain Kyle, also making him a member of the teaching team for Live Oak's primary weekend services. Kyle and Carey remained a part of the Live Oak ministry team until their departure in April 2006.

In 2005, Kyle and Carey attended the Onething young adult conference at the International House of Prayer (IHOP) in Kansas City, Missouri. This was a life-changing event for both and a major turning point in their ministry. Never before had either of them heard the truth of a God with a ravished heart for His bride, a God who is tender with us in the midst of our weakness, or a God who requires repentance but is quick to give grace when we approach Him with humility.

Shortly after returning to Lubbock from the conference, Kyle and Carey connected with the IHOP in Lubbock, a small ministry modeled closely after the Kansas City IHOP. After attending weekly prayer meetings for several months, Kyle eventually joined the volunteer staff. He served as a worship leader at the primary Tuesday night prayer meeting for nearly two years, taught regularly at IHOP weekend conferences, and served as director of the IHOP intern program. Kyle also served on the board of directors until moving to Fort Worth in June 2014.

Out of Kyle's time at IHOP came the vision for his current ministry passion, encounterGOD Ministries. Founded in November 2006, the primary vision of encounterGOD is to see followers of Jesus become extravagant lovers of God as the first commandment is restored to first place in the life of the church. In addition, encounterGOD embraces various justice initiatives, specifically in seeing abortion and human trafficking eradicated in the name and through the power of Jesus!

Kyle, Carey, and their two girls, Brooklyn and Ashtyn, make their home in Fort Worth, Texas.

For more information, or to book Kyle for a speaking engagement, please visit **www.kylemcnutt.com**.